MY MAM
SHIRLEY

JULIE SHAW

MY MAM SHIRLEY

THE TRUE STORY OF YORKSHIRE'S NOTORIOUS CRIMINAL FAMILY

HARPER
element

HarperElement
An imprint of HarperCollins*Publishers*
77–85 Fulham Palace Road,
Hammersmith, London W6 8JB

www.harpercollins.co.uk

and HarperElement are trademarks of
HarperCollins*Publishers* Ltd

First published by HarperElement 2014

3 5 7 9 10 8 6 4 2

© Julie Shaw and Lynne Barrett-Lee 2014

Julie Shaw and Lynne Barrett-Lee assert the moral right
to be identified as the authors of this work

A catalogue record of this book is
available from the British Library

PB ISBN: 978-0-00-754228-4
EB ISBN: 978-0-00-754229-1

Printed and bound in Great Britain by
Clays Ltd, St Ives plc

MIX
Paper from
responsible sources
FSC C007454

FSC™ is a non-profit international organisation established to promote the responsible management of the world's forests. Products carrying the FSC label are independently certified to assure consumers that they come from forests that are managed to meet the social, economic and ecological needs of present and future generations, and other controlled sources.

Find out more about HarperCollins and the environment at
www.harpercollins.co.uk/green

Echoes of My Past

A wall full of faces smile down on me,
And my heart begins to swell,
Past fuses with present so seamlessly,
Oh the stories these pictures could tell.

Old black and white memories are dancing,
Side by side with the colour of youth,
Hidden heartache temporarily halted,
By smiles that are clouding the truth.

Such happy times, such sad times,
Each inextricably linked to the last,
With spaces left for the future,
Amid these echoes of my past.

Note by the Author

My name is Julie Shaw, and my father, Keith, is the only surviving member of the 13 Hudson siblings, born to Annie and Reggie Hudson on the infamous Canterbury Estate in Bradford. We were and are a very close family, even though there were so many of us, and those of us who are left always will be.

I wanted to write these stories as a tribute to my parents and family. The stories are all based on the truth but, as I'm sure you'll understand, I've had to disguise some identities and facts to protect the innocent. Those of you who still live on the Canterbury Estate will appreciate the folklore that we all grew up with: the stories of our predecessors, good and bad, and the names that can still strike fear or respect into our hearts – the stories of the Canterbury Warriors.

ANNIE AND REGGIE HUDSON
Married 1919

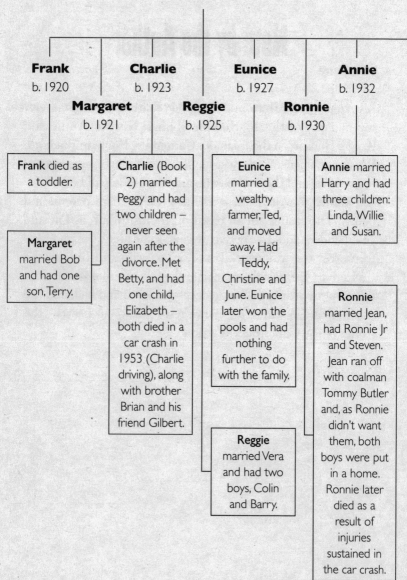

Frank
b. 1920

Margaret
b. 1921

Charlie
b. 1923

Reggie
b. 1925

Eunice
b. 1927

Ronnie
b. 1930

Annie
b. 1932

Frank died as a toddler.

Margaret married Bob and had one son, Terry.

Charlie (Book 2) married Peggy and had two children – never seen again after the divorce. Met Betty, and had one child, Elizabeth – both died in a car crash in 1953 (Charlie driving), along with brother Brian and his friend Gilbert.

Eunice married a wealthy farmer, Ted, and moved away. Had Teddy, Christine and June. Eunice later won the pools and had nothing further to do with the family.

Annie married Harry and had three children: Linda, Willie and Susan.

Reggie married Vera and had two boys, Colin and Barry.

Ronnie married Jean, had Ronnie Jr and Steven. Jean ran off with coalman Tommy Butler and, as Ronnie didn't want them, both boys were put in a home. Ronnie later died as a result of injuries sustained in the car crash.

Hudson Family Tree

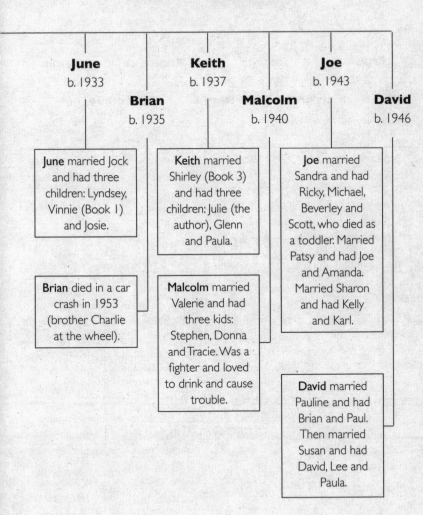

June
b. 1933

Keith
b. 1937

Joe
b. 1943

Brian
b. 1935

Malcolm
b. 1940

David
b. 1946

June married Jock and had three children: Lyndsey, Vinnie (Book 1) and Josie.

Keith married Shirley (Book 3) and had three children: Julie (the author), Glenn and Paula.

Joe married Sandra and had Ricky, Michael, Beverley and Scott, who died as a toddler. Married Patsy and had Joe and Amanda. Married Sharon and had Kelly and Karl.

Brian died in a car crash in 1953 (brother Charlie at the wheel).

Malcolm married Valerie and had three kids: Stephen, Donna and Tracie. Was a fighter and loved to drink and cause trouble.

David married Pauline and had Brian and Paul. Then married Susan and had David, Lee and Paula.

Prologue

Listerhills, Bradford, 1946

Shirley glared at the man who was sitting across the table from her; sitting, moreover, in her mam's chair. He was old and very tall and he was staring at her.

He leaned forward. 'You'll sit there all day, madam, if that's what it takes,' he said. 'But you *will* eat those sprouts and that's an end to it.' Then he sat back in her mam's chair and lit a cigarette. Shirley looked down at the disgusting green balls on her plate. No way was she eating them. Her mam wouldn't have made her eat them. Her mam had gone to work – she worked on the trolley buses and had left hours and hours ago – and if Shirley had to sit there till she came home, then she would.

Shirley couldn't quite believe her mam had gone and left her with this strange man in the first place. Normally when she went to work she'd leave her with her Granny Wiggins or her Auntie Edna, but then the man had turned up last night and they'd both sat Shirley down, with serious looks on their faces. 'This is your dad,' her mum had explained. 'He's come home from the war.'

Shirley didn't remember much about the war, but she knew she had a daddy and that he'd been in it, far across the sea, somewhere hot. He was called Raymond and her mam said he was going to be in charge now, which apparently included cooking all the meals when her mum was out at work and forcing her to eat things she hated.

Well, trying to. 'But I hate sprouts!' she protested again, hoping that he might get fed up of listening to her and allow her to leave the table so she could go and do something else. She still had to make her favourite dolly some new clothes.

'And I don't care,' he said, blowing smoke out of his mouth in a cloud that wafted across to her and made her nose wrinkle. 'Good food is hard to come by,' he added, 'and sprouts are very good for you. So you're not going to waste them. I'm your father and that's that.'

Shirley scowled at him. Two could play at that game. She folded her arms, started to swing her feet under her chair and counted sheep going over a wall in her head. She could count to a hundred now – her mam had taught her how to do it when she couldn't get to sleep at nights, and now it would help pass the time until she got back home from work.

As Shirley counted she stole glances at the man across the table. He had shiny stuff on his hair and the tops of some of his fingers were all yellow, and she decided she didn't like him one bit. She'd wanted him to be an uncle so she knew he'd go away again, or, if he wasn't, at least be nice like they always were. Her mam had brought home several uncles, all of them vastly preferable to the miserable-looking man in front of her, so if she *did* have to have one move in with her and her mam, why couldn't it have been one of them instead?

Not that she'd ever tell anyone. Her mam had warned her that she must never, ever mention the uncles, and because Shirley was a good girl she would do as she was told.

But she wasn't going to be a good girl when it came to eating sprouts. Her mam didn't make her eat them and this dad man wasn't going to either. So she was still sitting at the table when the sky grew dark outside and her mam finally got home from work.

With her back hurting and her bottom numb, Shirley was upset enough as it was when she saw her, but it was the parcel of chips her mother held in her hand that hit her hardest. She jumped down from the chair and immediately burst into tears.

'What's going on here?' her mother asked, immediately rushing across to scoop her up and embrace her.

'*He's* saying I have to eat these sprouts, Mam, and I won't! Tell him I don't like them!'

The man she was supposed to call 'Dad' was now squatting in front of the fire, a pair of wet socks dangling from his hands. He'd washed them in the sink earlier – her mam's stockings, too – while Shirley sat and glared at his back, and he had been in front of the fire drying them ever since. 'You rotten sod!' Shirley's mum snapped at him now, which made her feel better immediately. 'Don't you *dare* start laying the law down already, Raymond Read, or I'll have your guts for garters, you hear me? Your daughter doesn't like sprouts and she doesn't have to bloody well eat them!'

He stood up suddenly, making Shirley jump, and pointed at her mam. And Shirley knew it was very rude to point, as well. Not that he seemed to care. 'And don't *you* bloody undermine me, Mary!' he snapped, in his horrible deep voice. 'She's going to have to get used to me and we might as well start as we mean to go on. It's a bloody crime to waste food. There's people starving, in case you hadn't noticed, and this little madam chooses what she'll eat? Not on my watch.'

Shirley's mam let her back down to the floor again. 'Go on, love,' she said, patting her back. 'Go upstairs and get your nightie on. I'll put you some chips out, eh? Don't forget to wash your face, lovey. And behind your ears.'

Shirley scooted off as fast as she could, leaving her mam and dad shouting at each other. She'd still been in her mam's belly when her daddy had gone to be in the war, but she'd always told her he was a lovely, handsome soldier. Except he wasn't. He wasn't lovely at all, Shirley thought. She ran all the way up the stairs, clapping her hands over her ears to drown out the arguing. She didn't like that she'd have to 'get used to him', as he put it. She didn't like that he was set on making her eat things she didn't like.

She wriggled out of her dress and into her nightie and then went to wash her face and hands, as she'd been told. She knew she should try to look on the bright side her mam had told her about. She'd said her dad coming back might at least mean she'd get some brothers and sisters, and Shirley wanted brothers and sisters more than anything in the world.

So she could only hope than her mam had been telling her the truth. He definitely wasn't worth having on his own.

Chapter I

June 1958

Shirley and Anita burst through the front doors of St George's Hall into the warmth of the early evening air. Shirley couldn't remember the last time she'd felt so ecstatic. It was almost as if there was electricity running through her. She could certainly still feel the music throbbing away in her chest. But what she mostly couldn't believe was that she'd actually seen Cliff Richard in the flesh. She knew she'd never forget it ever – not as long as she lived.

'Oh, my good God, Shirl,' Anita cried, linking arms with her as they spilled out onto the pavement. 'I love him *so* much. Did you see how he danced? Did you *see?* God, them *hips!*'

'Trust you to be looking at his bloody hips, Anita!' Shirley scolded. 'What about his *voice?*' She sighed happily as they began to walk. 'I was far too busy singing along with him.'

He *was* sexy though. She had to admit that, even if it was only to herself.

'You bloody liar!' Anita huffed, reading her mind the way she always did. 'Far too busy, my eye!' She stopped on the pavement, then, allowing the throng of girls to stream around them. 'You know,' she said, freeing her arm and grabbing Shirley by both her shoulders suddenly. 'It's still really early, Shirl. It won't be dark for *hours* yet. *Please* say we don't have to go home just yet, eh? The Lister's is only a ten-minute walk away, after all. Let's go have a drink, eh? You're a single girl again now, don't forget.'

Yes, she was that, and she was determined to enjoy the freedom. Well, as much as she could; no, she didn't have a boyfriend stopping her from going out and having fun, but there was still her dad constantly on about her every frigging move – where she went, who she went with, when she was home.

It was all right for Anita. Her mam and dad were different. With two older brothers and a younger sister, she could get away with so much more, not least of which was the freedom to go out with who she wanted. And she did, too – she seemed to have a different boyfriend every week. But mostly Shirley envied her the freedom to *stay* out till she wanted, or at least a lot later than ten frigging p.m. How lovely it would be not to have your every move scrutinised. To be free.

Well, she *was* free in one way, at least. Free to daydream again. About marrying Cliff Richard and having a big house and lots of babies with him, even. She smiled to herself. You never knew, did you? And she was sure he'd caught her eye once or twice. No, she definitely wasn't ready to go home. She felt much more like dancing. Like Anita said, it wasn't even dark yet. The night, as they always said, was young.

She nodded. 'You're right. Why not? After all, I *am* single, aren't I?'

'*Exactly*. So you can do what you like,' Anita said, grabbing her hand and almost tugging her along the street.

'Well, sort of,' Shirley cautioned. 'Though we can't stay too long, Neet. You know what my bloody dad's like. He'll be on that doorstep, winding the clock up and threatening to bloody strangle me if I'm so much as a minute late.'

'Don't worry. I promise,' Anita said. 'We'll have you home on time, Cinderella. Can't have your dad turning into a pumpkin, can we?'

Shirley wasn't so sure that wouldn't be the best thing for him. He could certainly do with softening up.

For all that she railed against him being so ridiculously overprotective, Shirley had never really been one to disobey her father. Disgruntled as she'd been when he'd suddenly appeared in her young life, with all his funny ways and his rules and regulations, she'd soon realised home was a much more agreeable place if she came round to his way of thinking. She'd done this at first simply because she didn't want to get in his bad books but as time went on and she'd matured a bit, it was because she'd grown to love him. Yes, he was strict and orderly, and yes, he did have this idealistic image of her that she was always going to struggle to live up to, but he adored her and would go to the ends of the earth for her if she asked him to, and she loved that. In fact, sometimes, though she'd never have confessed it to anyone, she thought she loved him even more than her mam.

Not that Shirley didn't love her mam too, but Mary could be scary. She had a temper on her that was legendary both with the family *and* the neighbours. And once the family had been reunited, it soon became clear that, whatever went on before Shirley's dad went off to war, theirs was not the happiest of marriages. Her dad, it turned out, though always strong and determined, really wanted nothing more than a quiet life. But he didn't often get one, because Mary was not only very fiery, she was also insanely jealous. Shirley had never really understood why (and still didn't – particularly now she was older, and understood more about all those 'uncles') but it was as if her mam was constantly on guard against her dad being lured away by another woman.

Raymond wasn't even safe at work, it seemed. Once demobbed he'd got a job as a boiler firer at a big factory in Listerhills, but it seemed there was no peace for him there either. A regular occurrence in Shirley's childhood had been her mam constantly spying on him – she'd often turn up at the factory unannounced (Shirley herself sometimes in tow) to check if there were any women anywhere near making eyes at him. And if she got it into her head that he *might* have set his sights on someone, she'd think nothing of setting about him physically – either with her fists or anything else she could lay her hands on.

Shirley had spent much of her childhood not really understanding how it worked being a grown-up. As far as she'd been able to tell, her dad only loved two girls in the world: her and her mam. And her mam, in return, was always so horrible to him. How did that work? How could you love someone and be so horrible to them at the same time? Perhaps you couldn't, she'd come to realise, because, as the years went by, there were never any of the brothers and sisters they'd promised her when she was smaller – the one thing she'd always wanted more than anything in the world.

Yes, she'd had her dollies, who she'd loved and cared for with a passion, pushing them along in their shiny pram and dressing them in clothes she'd stitched for them herself. She also had her friends – and she'd make clothes for their dollies too – but at the end of every day no dolly could make up for going home alone; for being an only child in an unhappy home.

That was all she wanted as a child – a special friend, someone to play with, someone to go with on adventures, but mostly someone to be with when she was at home, who was in the same boat and could take her mind off the endless, endless arguing.

As it was, she'd spent her childhood stuck in the middle of a war that seemed almost as long and horrible as the one her dad had returned from. Every weekend, almost without fail, her parents, having gone out for a few drinks in the local, would come home and have the same old arguments: her mam accusing her dad of looking in the direction of another woman, and her dad telling her she needed her eyes testing. On and on it would go, usually till Raymond passed out drunk on the kitchen floor, at which point Mary would then yell for her from the bottom of the stairs.

'Shirley,' she'd screech up to her, loud enough to wake the dead, 'come down and help me get his head in the gas oven!'

Shirley never would, of course. She'd just cry and cry, and plead for her mam to leave her poor dad alone. 'That's it!' Mary would say then, dragging her coat round her shoulders. 'We're leaving home. And we're never coming back!'

Shirley remembered walking the streets with her mam for hours sometimes, however cold or wet it might be, and all she could hope was that when her mam finally sobered up enough to take her home, her dad would have taken himself to bed, so the whole cycle didn't start up again.

But at least it didn't last for ever. When Shirley was ten they'd moved to Clayton, on the outskirts of Bradford. It was the kind of village where everyone knew everyone else and looked out for one another as well, and Shirley soon became friendly with all the local children, as well as becoming popular with lots of young mums due to her love of helping out with their little ones.

But it was mainly better because she now had her Granny Wiggins living on the same street, and her Auntie Edna also living just a few doors further along – both places that provided a much-needed means of escape from the chilly atmosphere at home.

It was escape of another kind that had begun to occupy Shirley's mind as she'd entered her teens, however. She was counting the days till she could escape into her own life, which was going to be so different from the way it was now. She'd have her own home, her own husband and lots and lots of children. She would make her own wedding gown, and would float along the aisle in it, and have a ring put on her finger by a wonderful, loving man – Pat Boone or Elvis, perhaps, or that dreamy Tab Hunter. Or even – she sighed inwardly now, as his voice filled her head again – of her latest crush, the beautiful Cliff Richard, who could serenade her as he swept her off her feet.

The Lister's Arms was at the bottom of Manchester Road, and was currently the place all the young people went. She'd been a few times with John, her ex, but she always felt a little out of place there. It could be a rough place; lots of the lads from the Canterbury estate went there, so when she did go – with John, and latterly with Anita – they always tended to keep themselves to themselves.

'You go to the bar, Neet,' Shirley whispered as they walked into the busy pub. She'd never even tried to get served when she went in there, because she didn't look old enough by a mile yet. It was different for Anita, because her mam and dad let her wear make-up, so she'd been able to buy drinks since she was only 15.

It was yet another reason why Shirley couldn't wait for her eighteenth birthday. Anita nodded. She knew the drill. 'You grab some seats then, okay? Half of bitter?'

Shirley cast about then, trying to spot a couple of seats free in one of the corners, though it was difficult to see through the throng of people. Many were just standing chatting, but a few were gyrating to the sounds coming from the throbbing juke-box, and Shirley felt the familiar tug to get on the impromptu dance-floor and move to the music as well.

But then she spotted an empty table and rushed to bag it before it was taken, content for the moment to take in the atmosphere and marvel at the couples jiving and jitterbugging nearby.

'Guess who's propping up the bar?' Anita shouted above the din as she set down the two drinks on the table.

'Who?' Shirley asked, too far away to see over the crush of bodies.

'That Tucker Hudson. Remember? One of those brothers from over Canterbury.'

Shirley nodded as she sipped the head off her beer. She didn't really know the Hudson brothers, but she certainly knew *of* them. Knew they were best avoided, like pretty much everyone else did from her part of the world. She also knew the eldest one, Charlie, was back out of prison, and that he was the one you needed to avoid most of all, even if John had always talked about him like he was some sort of local hero.

She remembered that day she'd gone to court with John. It had seemed a strange thing to do then and it still felt strange now. All the cheering and chanting, and there being *so* many people, all to see someone sent down for doing something criminal – all there to *support* someone who her dad had said only got what he'd deserved. She'd never really understood that, even if John had tried to explain it to her. But then John had been friends with the Hudsons – one of the younger ones, anyway. Keith, was it? Yes, she was sure that was his name. The cocky, good-looking one. Till he'd gone and joined the army, at any rate.

'Which one?' she asked Anita, feeling suddenly fretful that if he was here, John himself might be in tonight as well. Which wasn't a problem, exactly, but she still didn't want to see him. Not so soon after finishing with him, anyway.

'Keith,' Anita confirmed, sitting down and shrugging her bag off her shoulder. 'The short one. Remember? He's in here with his sister. You know. Annie? Annie Jagger?'

Shirley shook her head, because she didn't think she did. She wished she was more like Anita, who always seemed to know everyone. But then she would, wouldn't she? She had two older brothers to go out with, after all.

'There,' Anita was saying now, as a record ended and the crowd parted briefly. 'See them now? She's the one with the platinum blonde hair.'

Shirley spotted them finally and then felt her face immediately flush; Keith Hudson was looking straight at her.

She lowered her gaze. *Now* she remembered him. And he'd hardly changed at all. Filled out a bit, even if he didn't look a great deal taller, and with the same arresting dark looks that she remember being so taken with before. John had noticed that too – she remembered that as well. He'd gone on about the two of them making eyes at each other – given her a pretty hard time about it, refusing to accept her denials. And now, having forgotten all about him these past two years, she realised those denials had been untrue. She risked raising her eyes again. He was still looking straight at her. Sizing her up. Almost willing her to hold his gaze.

'So?' she said to Anita, dropping her eyes again, feeling suddenly flustered. 'Why should I care who's in?'

'I didn't say you did care,' Anita answered. 'I was just saying, that was all. But now you mention it …' she added, glancing towards the bar and back again and grinning.

'Are we having a dance then, or what?' Shirley interrupted, twisting on the banquette so that she was facing more away from the bar now, feeling strangely uncomfortable under Keith Hudson's continuing scrutiny and still worried that John might be somewhere roundabouts as well.

'Hold your horses, Shirl!' Anita said. 'Let me have a slurp of this, at least. Ah, and don't look now, but guess who's coming over …'

Shirley turned around, expecting to see Keith Hudson striding towards her. But it wasn't. It was his sister, who looked like a mini Marilyn Monroe. It was a look lots of girls tried to emulate, but few managed to achieve. This one did, though. She was really very pretty.

But she also had the same sort of reputation her brothers had, if Anita was to be believed. 'Watch her, Shirl,' she whispered now. 'She's a bit of a wildcat.'

Not knowing quite what to make of that – what was she going to do? Attack them? – Shirley could only smile and make room on the banquette as the girl, who had that confident look of someone in her early twenties, marched up, said 'shove up' and plonked herself straight down between them.

She didn't speak at first either, but instead delved immediately into a capacious patent leather handbag, plucked out a pack of cigarettes and pulled one out with her teeth. She looked as though she might offer them round, and Shirley hoped she would. The rest of the girls there looked so sophisticated with their cigarettes hanging from their manicured fingers. But no, they quickly disappeared back into Annie's bag again.

She lit the cigarette using a shiny book of matches, and then took a long drag, carefully blowing out a series of smoke rings through her perfectly painted ruby lips.

Shirley watched in awe, wishing she could do something so clever. But, despite managing the odd secret practice, it was a skill that had so far eluded her. She would definitely have to pinch one of her dad's Capstans the next time she got a chance so she could practise some more.

Her entrance made, Annie Jagger turned towards her and smiled. Shirley smiled back nervously, wondering what exactly she'd come over for.

'My brother fancies you,' she said matter of factly, while tapping the end of her cigarette in the direction of the already over-flowing ashtray. She looked Shirley up and down then; not in a bitchy way, just as if she was working out whether she agreed with him.

'For some reason,' she then added, causing Shirley to revise her first interpretation. 'And he wants to take you out on a date.'

Shirley blinked at her. Fancy sending his bloody sister over to ask for him! So, for all his swagger, Keith Hudson was obviously not as brave as he liked to make out, then.

'Well, you can tell him no thank you,' she heard herself saying.

Annie Jagger drew on the cigarette again and blew some more smoke rings before answering. 'You still seeing *him*, then?' she asked finally. 'That John Arnold lad?'

'No,' Shirley began, shaking her head. 'We've split up.'

Annie Jagger nodded knowingly. 'I should think you would an' all, love! He's a wimp, he is, John Arnold. Why'd you want to go out with a wimp when you could be going out with a *proper* man?'

Shirley stared at her, bristling at the dismissive sneer on her face now. Bar pointing out that 'proper' men asked for their own dates, which she didn't dare to, she wasn't really sure how to respond to that. But it seemed she wasn't required to.

'A lad like our Keith,' Annie added, sending another inch of ash in the general direction of the ashtray, but missing and showering it on the table and over Shirley's skirt instead. 'A *proper* man, one who was off doing his bit for his country. While John bleedin' Arnold was hiding behind your flarey skirts, love!'

Now Shirley *really* didn't know what to say, and neither, it seemed, did Anita. She'd picked up her glass and was hiding as well – behind her beer. But, even as Shirley blushed, she felt a sudden rush of annoyance. No, he might not have been a fighter, but he wasn't hiding from anyone – not as far as she could tell, anyway – and at least he'd always behaved like a gentleman towards her. He'd always treated her like a lady, right from day one. Buying her flowers, buying her chocolates, holding doors open for her. So, yes, she might have grown a little bored with him, but that was *her* business, wasn't it? It certainly wasn't for anyone else to say. Wasn't for anyone else to be rude about him, either. Especially not this tiny little full-of-herself mouth on legs.

'I'll tell you what you can do,' Shirley said, pointedly brushing the ash off her skirt. It was her best one, and that annoyed her as well. 'You can go and tell your brother that I wouldn't go out on a date with him if he was the last man on earth.'

There was a heartbeat of silence, Anita looking on nervously, while Annie Jagger sat and glared at Shirley. She then scrunched out her half-smoked cigarette, raised her pencilled-in eyebrows and got to her feet. Shirley wondered if she should stand up as well, just to emphasise the difference in their heights, but then realised Keith's sister was no longer scowling but smiling. Not that Shirley intended to return the compliment and smile back. Who did she think she bloody was?

Annie laughed then. 'Ooh!' she said, stepping delicately out and round to the other side of the table. 'Game on, then, it is, love? Well, let's see how long you can resist the Hudson charm, shall we?'

And with that, she sauntered back to her brother at the bar, hips wiggling suggestively as she picked her way through the dancers, soaking up the admiring glances that she was obviously used to gathering, like she was a magnet for every male eye in the room.

It came into Shirley's head then. The words John had used two years back. He'd got quite cross, too – the day after they'd been in court, it was. Said her and Keith Hudson's eyes had been just like a pair of magnets. And she'd had to say again and again and again just how ridiculous he was being. And then Keith Hudson had simply disappeared out of her life. And that had been that. Gone and forgotten.

But if that were so, why was she finding it so hard right now not to follow Annie Jagger's progress back to her brother, just for her eyes to land again, however fleetingly, on his?

'Jesus Christ, Shirley!' Anita was spluttering, dragging her attention back. 'It's a wonder she didn't clock you one! She's a nutcase, she is!'

'I don't bloody care,' Shirley said, picking up her glass and gulping a mouthful of beer down. Her fingers were trembling, which annoyed her even more. 'She's not laying down the law to *me*!' she huffed as she set it down. 'I have more than enough of that at home, thanks.' She then picked up the glass again and downed the rest of the beer in a couple of swallows, before banging it more heavily onto the table. She had no idea if she was being watched but she bloody hoped so, just so she could press her point home and ignore them. 'Come on, Anita,' she said, all appetite for dancing now gone, not to mention the dreamy post-Cliff euphoria. 'It's getting late and I'm tired. We're off home.'

'But it's only –' Anita began protesting.

'You stay if you like,' Shirley said, leaving the table, 'but I'm going home. I'm not staying here to be told who I should or shouldn't be seeing. The cheek of her!'

Anita grabbed the cardigan she'd not long taken off and hurriedly shoved her arms into it as she followed Shirley out, via the far side of the dance-floor.

'You all right?' she asked Shirley. 'Don't let it get to you. Just take no notice.'

'Oh, I will be. And I won't! Who do those bloody Hudsons think they are?'

It was a thought she kept thinking for the entire 45-minute walk home, of necessity. As was their impromptu Cliff Richard and the Drifters sing-along – to quell the butterflies that were now dancing in her stomach.

Chapter 2

Shirley's dad was in a worse mood than she'd seen in a long time. 'One of those Hudson boys?' he snapped at her. 'Them from Little Horton? You're bloody well not going out with him, and that's that!'

It was nearly six o'clock and Shirley knew she'd have Keith knocking on the door any minute. And her mam hadn't even finished pinning up her hair yet. 'Mam, *tell* him!' she said indignantly. 'I'm 17 now *and* I'm working, so I should be allowed to go out with who I like!'

Though now she was wishing she hadn't even told them. Well, wishing she hadn't told her dad, at any rate. Her mam had been fine. But as for her dad … well, that had been something of a revelation. She never imagined in a million years that her dad even knew who the Hudsons were – he hardly ever left Clayton except to go to work, after all. But as soon as she'd said the name and where they came from, he'd gone berserk. The family's reputation must have been even greater than she'd realised.

'What's wrong with being from Little Horton?' Shirley's mam tried on her behalf.

'Yes, *exactly*,' Shirley added. 'Dad, you're just being a snob.'

'Everything!' Raymond barked, all the veins in his neck bulging. 'It's that bloody Charlie Hudson's brother from Canterbury, that's who it is! How the bloody *hell* did you get mixed up with the likes of him?'

'There's nothing *wrong* with him!' Shirley began, as her mam tried to finish her hair off. Not that easy when she was finding it almost impossible to keep still. 'He's –'

'So *you* say,' her father carried on, talking right over her. 'Oh, *I* know how this has happened,' he said suddenly, waggling a finger in her direction. 'It's that bloody Anita's fault, isn't it? It's her got you mixed up with them, isn't it? That friend of yours is never happy unless she's gallivanting around the bloody town, that one!'

'Why do you *always* blame Anita?' Shirley shouted back, rising from the table. If there was one thing that annoyed her more than any other criticism, it was having it suggested that she didn't make her own decisions. Actually, no – it was worse than that. What was really annoying was his suggestion that she let her best friend make them for her. The cheek! 'It's got *nothing* to do with Anita, Dad,' she fumed. 'I'm not a baby, you know! I make up my own mind. And I've made up my own mind about going out with Keith Hudson, so there!'

But he didn't seem to be listening. 'So *you* say,' he huffed, marching back and forth across the front-room carpet, craning his neck every so often to look out into the street. 'But she never liked that John of yours, did she? It's all falling into place now. Is that why you've blown him out all of a sudden?' He ran his hand through his hair, trying to haul the disobedient curls back into place. 'And for one of them bleeding Hudson repro-bates as well. Hell-*fire*, Shirley! You can do better than that.'

Shirley sat and fumed, cursing her honesty. She shouldn't have told him. It was as simple as that. She should have lied, like so many other girls did, about where they were going, what they were doing and who they were doing it with – and for precisely the reason she was cursing herself now; because some fathers so obviously couldn't see reason themselves. Who was her dad to say what Keith Hudson was like? He'd never even met him! Just listened to gossip and taken it as gospel, that was what, and now she was stuck with the distressing possibility that Keith would turn up and immediately be sent packing.

The thought was mortifying and she wished she'd been altogether more crafty – sneaked out while he was looking the other way. As it was, he was very much *in* her way, seemingly determined to ruin everything, and she needed her mam to help her try to get him to see reason. Though if he didn't, she decided, she was going out with Keith Hudson anyway, hook or by crook, whether her dad liked it or not. He wouldn't wait around for ever, after all.

Up to now, it had to be said, Keith Hudson had been impressively patient. Well, perhaps persistent was the better word, Shirley decided, and she decided she liked that a lot. She had no idea what his sister had reported of their conversation at the Lister's a fortnight previously, but she had a hunch – given what Anita had told her about Annie – that she would have repeated it verbatim. Probably would have enjoyed doing so as well, Shirley reckoned, given the mischievous gleam she'd had in her eye.

But whatever the facts, two other facts had subsequently become clear – that she couldn't seem to get Keith Hudson out of her mind and that, even if she had, he'd have popped straight back in again, because he'd certainly been popping up in person. It felt like he'd been everywhere these past couple of weeks, showing up when least expected; he'd suddenly started going to Farmer Giles's coffee bar – where she and Anita often hung out when they were bored – and he'd turned up for the Saturday matinee at the picture house, too. He'd even been waiting outside the sewing factory Shirley worked at. She'd come out after her shift on the previous Monday and there he'd been, large as life – well, actually, not so large in Keith's case – casually leaning against the bus stop, smoking a cigarette.

'You again?' she'd said, trying to come across as offhand but failing miserably, as the colour tracked up her cheeks and her stomach danced a jig. 'You're like a bloody bad penny, you are,' she added, 'always showing up. Haven't you got anything better to do?'

She waved off her work friends, who were all in danger of getting the giggles and embarrassing her even further. Then she stood in front of him, conscious of his lingering, up-and-down look.

He grinned. He had the nicest smile ever, she decided, with his beautifully straight white teeth and the slight dimple in his chin. He shrugged his shoulders. 'Can't blame a bloke for trying, can you? Anyway, you'll have to walk me home or you'll be responsible for me losing half a week's wages.'

Shirley shook her head in confusion. 'And how exactly do you work that out?'

'Well,' Keith explained, 'our Annie bet me a pound that you were too much of a snob to let a tyke like me take you out, and I really can't afford to lose a pound, Shirley.' He winked. 'So you'll have to take pity on me, won't you?'

She'd refused, though. Same as she'd refused on the Tuesday and Wednesday, but then on the Thursday night, when she'd gone out with Anita to the Ideal Dance-hall and he'd turned up there as well, she'd finally succumbed to the feeling in her tummy that, try as she might to ignore it, simply wouldn't go away.

'Yes, *okay* then!' she'd almost huffed at him, after his casual announcement that she really didn't know what she was missing. Because that was the problem; she was beginning to think she *did* know. Or, at least, that she was very keen to find out, however much it galled her to know Annie blinking Hudson was obviously right about her falling for the legendary Hudson charm.

There was also the issue of the pound she'd owe her brother, which Shirley reckoned served her right. So they'd made arrangements for Keith to bring her back there on the Saturday night, when there was a band playing that she liked.

The intervening 48 hours had felt like the longest in Shirley's life, as if time had slowed down especially to annoy her. And now, at the eleventh hour, with him due to knock on the door at any minute, her blasted dad could go and ruin everything.

He was beyond angry now. She could tell. He'd just said 'bleeding' and he never said that word unless he was about to blow a fuse. And the thought of him blowing a fuse at Keith Hudson was unthinkable. He'd run a mile and probably never come back. Probably think she wasn't worth the trouble after all.

Shirley decided to change her tack. Perhaps taking him on wasn't the best way of going about things. '*Please*, Dad,' she begged, softening both her voice and her expression. 'Keith's not like his brothers. Honestly, he isn't. He's really nice and he'll be here calling for me in ten minutes. *Please* don't show me up, Dad. I couldn't bear it.'

Shirley's mam had picked up a tin of lacquer and was now spraying the Tony Curtis quiff she'd created in Shirley's hair. 'Raymond, leave the lass alone,' she said, as the can hissed around her. 'I *mean* it. She does right playing the field for a bit instead of getting herself tied down to the first man she meets. How else is she going to meet mister right?'

There was a heavy emphasis on the 'right' bit, but Shirley's dad didn't seem to notice.

'Playing the field?' he said, leaping up from the chair he'd only just sat back down on. 'No daughter of *mine* is going to play the bloody field! Them Hudsons are trouble, do you hear me? That Charlie's just out from the clink for God knows what, and that younger one – Malcolm, is it? – he's another one. Locked up more often than he's out, as well! They're *all* bloody trouble, and everyone knows it! You're not going anywhere with a bleeding Hudson boy and that's an end to it!'

Just as Shirley was about to point out that they weren't *all* bloody trouble, there was a soft but clearly audible knock on the front door. 'Oh, Mam,' she cried, the injustice of it making tears prickle in her eyes now, 'look at him! You've got to go and stop him, Mam, please!' She desperately hoped that the closed front door was enough to contain the commotion that was going on inside.

Because it certainly looked as if he was going to need stopping. He was already rolling up his shirt sleeves as he stomped off to answer the door. What was he going to do? Punch poor Keith in the face just because of his surname? Shirley blanched at the thought. He wouldn't do that, surely? 'Mam!' she said again, panicked now, because she'd never seen her dad like this before. 'Hurry up. *Stop* him. He might *hit* him!'

Mary took a hankie from her pinny pocket and passed it to her, seemingly unruffled. 'Here, love, buck up – don't spoil your lovely make-up. You know your dad – his bark's always worse than his bite, and he's not going to do any such thing. He wouldn't dare, because he knows he'll have me to answer to, doesn't he? Come on, let's go and meet this young man of yours, shall we?'

Shirley sniffed and carefully dabbed the corners of her eyes before following her mam out into the hall, feeling slightly reassured. She could only just see Keith because he was half hidden beyond her dad, but she could see enough to catch the fact that he was smiling politely and had stuck out a hand ready for shaking.

'Nice to meet you, Mr Read,' he was saying. 'I've heard a lot about you. And I also want to promise you that I'll have your Shirley back early – I'll walk her all the way back home myself.'

Shirley could tell, just from the back of him, what her dad's expression would be. 'I'd expect nothing less, lad,' he answered. 'But don't get ahead of yourself. Unless I'm very much mistaken, I haven't even said she can go yet, have I?'

Shirley's heart sank as she watched her dad physically bristle. He wasn't going to send him packing now, was he? She bristled herself. If he did she'd certainly let him know all about it – how he had comprehensively, *totally* ruined her entire life. But it seemed he was still busy giving his lecture. 'Oh, I've heard a lot about *you*, as well, lad,' he growled. 'You *and* the rest of your family.'

This didn't seem to faze Keith at all. 'I can't speak for the rest of the clan, obviously,' he said, standing straight on the doorstep, as if to attention. 'But I can assure you that I've never been in trouble with the law. In fact, sir, I've been in the army, just like you.'

Shirley cringed in anticipation of her dad's likely response to this. The war had been years ago but that didn't mean he was going to let anyone forget it, least of all the 21-year-old currently standing on his doorstep, who she knew, even though her dad still had his back to her, would now be at the end of a particularly stony glare. 'Like *me*?' he barked. 'I wasn't messing around "in the army", as you put it. I was fighting for my country, lad! Crawling through bloody ditches in Burma and getting stabbed by the bloody Japs! So you're wrong there, my son. You weren't *just* like me at all!'

Keith nodded his acknowledgement and Shirley's mam, unseen by her dad, nudged her arm and rolled her eyes. 'No, you're right, sir,' Keith quickly corrected. 'Not the same thing at all. I just mentioned it because I'm honoured to meet a war hero, honest I am.' He cleared his throat and for the first time let his gaze rest momentarily on Shirley. 'I would also be honoured,' he went on, smiling at Shirley's mam as well now, 'if you'd give me a chance to prove that I'm a good man, Mr Read, and to allow me to court your daughter.'

Shirley felt a smile form on her lips as Keith looked at her. Her mam smiled as well. Then poked her dad in the kidneys with a very forceful finger, making it clear that, to her mind, Keith had done what he'd needed to – proved that he wasn't a reprobate at all.

Shirley held her breath. How could her father find any reason to turn him down? He was smart, he was polite and he couldn't be held responsible for his surname. On those grounds alone, it was only fair that her dad agreed. And it seemed he *did* agree. 'Right then,' he said finally, 'all right. She can go. *But* –' he added, raising an admonishing finger, 'I'm warning you, lad, I'll be at this front door at ten o'clock sharp, and if Shirley isn't walking through it, you are *bang* in trouble. Understand?'

Shirley was out of the house like a rocket.

'Phew,' she said as they rounded the corner onto Bradford Road. 'That was touch and go there for a minute, wasn't it? But you did *so* well.'

The night was young, the air was warm and she was going on a date with Keith Hudson. She felt such a surge of excitement at being out with him finally that it was all she could do not to skip down the street.

He stuck out an elbow for Shirley to slip her arm into, and winked. 'You don't grow up in a family like mine without learning a few things,' he said, grinning at her. 'Like how to get yourself out of a sticky situation. And trust me, Shirl, your dad's a pussycat compared to mine.'

A pussycat? Shirley smiled back at Keith as they walked, feeling a little shy all of a sudden, not to mention a bit bemused by what he'd said. Pussycat wasn't the kind of word she'd have used to describe her dad – not when he was angry, at any rate. He was more like a frigging bull at a gate, in her book.

But not to Keith, obviously. What was *his* dad like, then? She'd have a chance to find out soon enough, she supposed, and in the meantime the thought that Keith wasn't afraid of hers sent another thrill running through her. How nice to have a fearless man on her arm for a change. Even though she hadn't realised it at the time, she'd obviously done right to break up with boring John Arnold. So that a proper man like Keith – home from the army, no less – could come back into her life and sweep her off her feet.

Whatever his surname happened to be.

Chapter 3

Shirley loved going to the Ideal. A purpose-built dance-hall in the same car park as the Red Lion pub in Bankfoot, it was her and Anita's favourite of all the dance-halls; the place where you could always be sure of a night spent bopping to the latest sounds. It was owned by a local man called Bert Shultz. Bert was only in his late twenties, but everyone knew him – chiefly because he'd lived comfortably off his wealthy parents' money all of his young life and wasn't ashamed of it, either; he made no secret of the fact that the Ideal was a gift for him from his mother.

This didn't go down well with everyone – not at first, anyway. Especially the young local lads, who believed men should look after themselves. But they tolerated him, because in the main he kept out of their business and, whatever anyone had to say about him, he certainly knew *his* – he always put on a good night.

During the week, Bert would provide entertainment by way of a free juke-box, but at the weekends he moved things up a gear. Local skiffle groups would come along and play songs from the current hit parade, and the dance-floor would really come alive.

Shirley loved going dancing at the Ideal more than almost anything. Loved the atmosphere, loved the sense of excitement and anticipation, loved the way all the girls would sit demurely along one side of the dance-floor while all the boys stood along the other side – eyeing them and trying to pluck up the courage to ask them for a dance. She loved that young people from all over Bradford would be there; that sense that you were at the place everyone most wanted to be. And mostly, if she wasn't dancing herself, she loved to watch. Loved watching how the couples would look as though they'd come straight out of the movies once they stepped out onto the dance-floor, the men so handsome in their long drape jackets, with their coloured collars and suede brothel creepers, and the girls in their ballet pumps, their circular skirts flying as they pirouetted around to Bill Haley and Buddy Holly. It was magical to watch, and looked magical to do, as well, and though Shirley was happy enough dancing with Anita – John Arnold had never been much of a dancer – how she had ached to be in the arms of a lad so she could properly put into practice all those hours she'd spent secretly learning how to jive with a kitchen chair.

And now she had one. Well, she hoped so. If Anita was to be believed, anyway. Knowing everything about everyone, she assured Shirley that Keith loved to bop and that only last week she'd seen him jiving away with his sister.

The walk to Bankfoot took them a good half an hour, but it was a lovely early summer's evening and they passed the time chatting about what they'd been up to during the day. Keith was dressed in typical Teddy Boy attire and, from the musky smell she kept catching off him, had dabbed on some after-shave as well, and she was pleased that her new boyfriend had gone to so much effort.

'Come on then, kiddo,' he said, grinning as they finally approached the entrance. 'Let's go show 'em how it's done, shall we? Though hang on,' he added, glancing first down at Shirley's black pumps and then at her bag, 'you're not going to pull a pair of high heels out of that handbag of yours, are you? Only you're two inches taller than me already, and I don't want to look stupid.'

Shirley smiled politely, and though she couldn't have cared less about his height, immediately and instinctively tried to lower her shoulders. 'Don't worry. I don't like wearing high heels much,' she lied, pleased at her foresight in choosing to put the flats on her feet, rather than one of the pairs of kitten heels she often wore for dancing. It made her smile to herself, even so. Here he was, so concerned about appearances and everything, yet the Teddy Boy suit he was currently sporting was so obviously a couple of sizes too big. In fact – and she stifled a giggle at the thought – at first sight, seeing Keith turn up in it had put her a little bit in mind of Norman Wisdom. But the impression had disappeared almost as quickly as it had formed. No, despite his size, Keith Hudson was *nothing* like Norman Wisdom. There was a glint in his dark eyes that was *nothing* like Norman Wisdom's. Something so manly. Something so sexy.

He was the best-looking lad she'd ever been out with, in fact, and being led into the Ideal on his arm – this lad from the notorious Canterbury estate, no less – made her feel ever so slightly weak at the knees. She could only hope they'd hold up once she was properly in his arms so she didn't go down like a sack of potatoes.

Bert Shultz was on the door, wearing the same thing he wore every weekend: black suit and dicky bow. He nodded his usual greeting at Shirley, and seemed happy enough to take the two shillings Keith proffered for their entrance, but at the same time he narrowed his eyes. 'Evening, lad,' he said, dropping the money into his cash box. 'I don't want any of your shenanigans tonight, do you hear? Some of the other lads from your end are here tonight,' he elaborated, 'and I've already had to eject a couple of them. Best behaviour tonight, lad, okay?'

Shirley turned, expecting Keith to nod politely at this, but instead he walked straight inside, dragging Shirley in his wake, and offering a mild, 'Get lost, Bert,' as he did so.

Shirley gaped. 'But –'

'I can't stick that stuck-up get,' Keith said, once they were out of earshot. 'I don't know who he thinks he's talking to.'

Shirley felt a nervous flutter of excitement in her stomach. It was a feeling she was beginning to become more than a little familiar with; a feeling that was becoming synonymous with being around her new, rather dangerous-seeming boyfriend. She'd never tell her mam and she surprised herself by admitting it, but it was a feeling she liked rather a lot. 'I know!' she agreed gaily, as he led her into the dance-hall. 'What a bloody toff he is, isn't he?'

Keith tightened his grip on her arm and returned her smile with a wink, and soon they were making their way across the crowded dance-floor towards the gang of people already hanging around the bar area. Not that it was a bar in the usual sense of the word. There was no alcohol served in the Ideal Dance-hall – not to anyone. So sarsaparillas and milkshakes were the order of the day. Hardly any of the girls minded; they were there for the dancing – but with some of the other dance-halls selling alcohol these days, for the older lads it was a real bone of contention.

Not that they couldn't get hold of some if they wanted it. For those in need of a bit of Dutch courage, there was always the Red Lion next door, the pub which Bert Shultz's parents owned, and in whose car park the Ideal had been built. So the older lads would usually get a pass-out from Bert during the band breaks (or as often as they felt thirsty), down as many pints as they could afford and then come back in again, better placed to chat up any girls they'd had their eye on and – assuming they could still stand up reasonably straight – hit the dance-floor again. For fear of any drunken uprisings that might follow, Bert had no choice but to encourage it as, after all, it was money in his parents' pockets.

'Hey up, Shirley,' Keith said, pointing to where two lads were standing at the far end of the bar. 'There's Bobby and Titch – sorry, my mates Bobby Moran and Titch Williams. Let's go stand with them for a bit, shall we?'

Shirley's face fell. For one thing, wasn't Keith planning on getting her a drink? And for another, she wasn't sure she wanted to go and stand with them anyway. She'd seen the one Keith called Titch a few times before, and he was bad enough – loud and raucous and loved to think he was a bit of a ladies' man (which he wasn't) – but Bobby Moran was much worse. He looked a good few years older than Keith and she'd seen him around several times, and every time he'd been drunk and staggering around the place. He liked to fight, too – Anita had told her that before, and if she was honest, she found him rather scary. 'Do we have to?' she asked Keith. 'That Bobby gets right on my nerves.'

Keith laughed and carried on walking across the dance-floor, which was currently half empty, as the band hadn't started yet. 'Oh, he's all right really,' he reassured her. 'Once you get to know him. He fancies my big sister, Margaret, you know. Had a right crush on her, he did.'

'But isn't she in her thirties?' Shirley asked him, bewildered by this.

Keith laughed. 'Well into,' he said. 'But that didn't stop her going on a date with him once – strictly out of pity, of course,

Julie Shaw

but he's never stopped going on about it ever since. Still can't understand why she married her Bob and not him.'

Shirley followed Keith, as there didn't seem much else to be done. 'Well, I obviously don't know anything about Bob,' she whispered, as Bobby Moran raised an arm and waved at them, 'but I imagine your sister made the right choice.'

She meant it, too; Keith's friends looked like they'd come to the Ideal straight from a jumble sale – well, via the Red Lion, of course. Bobby Moran was wearing a funny little hat that wouldn't have looked out of place on Charlie Chaplin, and the other one – Titch Williams – was in a blue drape jacket with a black collar, which wouldn't have been too bad on its own – well, if it had fitted him – except that sticking out of the bottom were a pair of horrible brown trousers.

Titch wolf-whistled as they reached them, looking her up and down as he did so. 'You've done all right for yourself, young Hudson,' he said, treating Shirley to the sort of smile that made it clear he thought his get-up was the bees knees, even if no one else did. 'She looks like bleeding Betty Boop!' he added brightly.

Shirley wasn't sure whether this was supposed to be a compliment or an insult, though she *was* sure of one thing; that this wasn't quite how she expected her and Keith's first date to be panning out. She hoped it wasn't indicative of how the rest of it was going to go. Nothing to drink, and having to stand around with a pair of gawping idiots. Where was the romance in that?

'Leave her alone, Titch, or I'll bleeding bop you one,' Keith said, equally brightly. 'Anyway, where's your birds, then? Mislaid them somewhere, have you?'

Shirley stood by Keith, keeping her arm tucked in the crook of his, and wondered what sort of girls would want to go out with either of them. 'As it happens,' Titch answered, puffing himself up importantly, 'Jayne Mansfield was tied up tonight and I told Doris Day I was having a night in. Thought I'd come and check out some local talent for a change.'

'Course you did,' Keith said, squeezing Shirley's arm. 'And fortunately for the rest of us, the local talent know an ugly little bleeder when they see one.'

This little quip seemed to invoke some sort of laddish primeval instinct, because she was then forced to step aside as the three of them started shadow boxing with each other, and right in the middle of the bar queue as well. She scanned the room, hoping that Anita might be in too, but she wasn't – not yet, anyway. And this wasn't at *all* the sort of night out she'd had in mind with her new boyfriend.

Perhaps reading her thoughts, Keith stopped messing about with his friends and finally got her a milkshake but, to her surprise, ordered nothing for himself. Did that mean he was sloping off to the Red Lion now? If so, what was she supposed to do?

'Aren't you having a drink?' Shirley asked him. She sincerely hoped he wasn't about to up and leave her there.

He shook his head. 'Nah,' he said. 'I'll get one in a bit. Later on, once I've got a bit of money.'

Shirley felt dismayed all over again. Didn't he have enough money *now*? Had he really come out with only enough money to pay for them both to get in and buy one measly drink? She wasn't sure what to do – she did have a few bob of her own tucked into her bag, but she hadn't expected to have to spend it. And he might be offended if she suggested it, anyway. 'I've got enough for us both to have one,' she decided to suggest anyway, wondering where he imagined he might be getting this 'bit of money' from, exactly.

Keith shook his head a second time. 'Don't need it,' he said, smiling. 'Thanks, but no thanks. Just wait a bit – till the band gets going – and then I'll have plenty. Just wait and see.'

The band duly started and the floor began filling up. 'Come on,' Keith said. 'It's the Four Pennies. I like this one, don't you?'

Shirley didn't have a clue what he was on about, but now the music was playing and they were up and dancing along to it, she didn't care. They danced to that song, then the next, then jived to Buddy Holly, and, at last, she felt entirely in her element. Anita had been right – Keith really was good enough to show them how it was done, and before long she was aware that a space had cleared around them, not so much to watch, exactly, just to give them sufficient room. And she was loving it, feeling a million dollars in the lemon blouse and polka-dot skirt she'd made herself, loving the way the colours blurred into one as she danced, and the swish of the frilly underskirt that peeked from under the hem. Loving how, when Keith sent her into a spin, it mushroomed out so prettily all around her. But what she most loved was how Keith was such a brilliant, brilliant dancer and how she was getting such envious looks from all the other girls. Keith Hudson, she realised, must be a bit of a catch.

All good things had to come to an end, however, and when she spied Bobby Moran waving at them both about half an hour later, she knew their turn on the dance-floor was done. At least for the moment. 'Quick!' Keith whispered to her as Bobby acknowledged that he'd seen him. 'What's your favourite song?'

Shirley was confused. 'Um, er … I don't know. Why? What do you mean?'

'Your favourite singer? Your favourite song? Both, if you like. What is it?'

'Um ...' Shirley began, wondering what the hell was going on. 'Er, how about "Why" by Anthony Newley?' she suggested. 'But Keith, why d'you want to know, anyway?'

Keith grinned at her. 'Right then,' he said, not answering her question. 'You go stand over there and you'll see.'

'Over where? And what about you? Where are you going, then?'

'Go on. Go over by Titch,' he said nudging her in the general direction. 'Don't worry. I won't be long.' Then, to her dismay, Shirley found herself left alone in the middle of the dance-floor as her new date turned around and marched off.

What the hell's going on? She thought crossly as she stomped back towards the bar. Titch, indeed. What kind of a name was that, anyway? Yes, he was tiny – really tiny – but he had a not-at-all titchy nose. Which looked like it was broken. And though she was willing to concede that he had a friendly enough smile, she was in no mood to be friendly in return. 'What's Keith's bloody game?' she demanded when she reached him.

Titch laughed. And that was another thing. Why did they all seem to find everything so funny? Why did there seem to be this permanent joke that she wasn't allowed in on? 'Hark at you!' he said, apparently not remotely concerned to have her scowling at him. 'You sound like one of them posh birds off the films. Keep yer knickers on, love. He'll be back soon enough.'

He nudged her as well. Then he pointed towards the stage, where the band were setting up and testing their sound, and where – to Shirley's horror – Keith was standing now as well, holding a microphone. What was he *doing* up there? She couldn't imagine anything more excruciating. Standing up there, with everyone staring. But, from the look of him, he didn't seem to be self-conscious at all. They were obviously about to start performing as well, because the music from the juke-box was starting to fade out.

'Is he going to *sing*?' she asked his friend, but the question was answered before he could. Keith was indeed going to sing. In fact, he was already singing. Singing 'Why' by Anthony Newley.

Crooning the words, he smiled down at the growing cluster of girls at the front. The room had fallen silent, and those who had been dancing were now shuffling towards the stage, forming a semi-circle at the front.

Good grief, Shirley's thought, her mouth hanging open as she listened. He sang even better than most of her favourite singers, Cliff included. How had she not *known* this about him? How come he hadn't said? She was so shocked, she even found herself smiling at Titch. 'Shall we go up there to watch?' she asked, feeling a sudden urgent need to get to the front herself, so that he could sing to *her*.

'Sure,' he said, leading the way proprietorially as they threaded through the crowd. And it *was* a crowd, too. Keith Hudson was obviously very popular. He was definitely popular with Shirley right now. In fact she was almost bursting with pride at this new boyfriend of hers. Just getting up on stage and singing like that! Imagine! She couldn't have done anything like that in a million years. And nor, more to the point, could John Arnold. And as they reached the front, Keith immediately began to sing directly at her.

He could have carried on in that vein all night, Shirley decided, but the song came to an end and his turn on the stage was obviously done, to a deafening round of applause. Keith was obviously popular; Shirley noticed that his other friend, Bobby Moran, had taken off his silly hat and was now walking among the crowd, holding it out, and that they were actually putting coins into it as well. 'Is that for Keith?' she asked Titch, already half-knowing the answer.

'What else do you think they'd be doing it for?' he replied, as if she was mad. 'Sings like a nightingale, our Tucker does, doesn't he? That's how it works, love. Bit for him, bit for Bobby – bit for me an' all; he'll always stand me a drink or two.'

Shirley found this 'Tucker' thing as bemusing as she ever had. She recalled John Arnold telling her about it when they'd first got together; how all the Hudson boys, from Charlie down, had *always* been known as Tucker, and that it wasn't complicated, because there was only one 'top' Tucker on the streets at any time, and if there was another, they were simply 'young Tucker'.

But why 'Tucker' anyway? She made a mental note to ask Keith sometime. He had so many brothers and sisters she was already all at sea without them all being called the same thing as well.

'Don't you worry,' Titch continued, patting Shirley's arm with a clammy hand. 'He'll treat you as well. Course he will. His little posh bird.'

This brought Shirley up short. If there was one thing she hated more than her father telling her she didn't know her own mind, it was anyone – *anyone* – referring to her as that. It had irritated her almost all her life. She had even been teased about it at school in Clayton, and it was simply because she was an only child and had that bit more than her friends with lots of siblings. 'I'm not a bloody posh bird!' she snapped. 'I'm just the same as the rest of you.'

Titch laughed out loud. 'Yeah, course you are, love. And if me auntie had balls, she'd be me uncle.'

'I am not posh!' she persisted. Who was he to tell her what she was or wasn't?

'Where d'you live, then?' he said.

What did that have to do with it? 'Clayton,' she huffed.

Titch swept his arm down and across his body and bowed his head for good measure. 'Then I rest my case, Your Majesty. Anyway, there's nowt wrong with posh. You want to have some pride in where you've come from, lass, you do.'

Shirley didn't know about that – it wasn't as if she wasn't proud of where she came from, exactly. She just didn't want people making assumptions about her all the time, thinking she was stuck up and unapproachable when she wasn't.

And tonight, in her new role as Keith 'Tucker' Hudson's 'bird', she suddenly felt like flavour of the month. She didn't really know why, but she felt as if she'd suddenly been granted membership of an exclusive club. Once Keith had brought soft drinks for her and all his friends, and been congratulated by one and all – especially the girls – it began to feel like she'd known everyone for ever; girls and lads she'd never met before being so welcoming and friendly as, one by one, Keith introduced her to everyone. And it really felt as if he *knew* everyone, as well.

The atmosphere was great, the music was great and, by the time the band broke again, she found she didn't even mind when he said he'd be nipping over to the Red Lion for a bit.

'I won't be long,' he promised. 'An' it'll give you a chance to get to know some of the girls. I'll just have a quick pint and I'll be back before you know it.'

Shirley wasn't a nervous girl, in fact she loved nothing more than meeting new people and joining in, despite being an only child. Or perhaps because of it. She'd had a lifetime of practice in having to make friends. Even so, she didn't want him running away with the idea that she'd be standing for any nonsense. She was never going to be like her mam, treating her dad like some sort of criminal for so much as speaking to another female, but she wasn't having him thinking she was a pushover, either. 'Okay,' she said, nodding, 'but don't leave me too long. Don't forget I have to be home for ten and my dad'll be waiting for me.'

'Ten minutes,' he promised, planting a kiss on each of her cheeks in turn. Would tonight be the night when he properly kissed her? She hoped so. And as he headed off out of the front doors with Titch Williams and Bobby Moran, she caught another lingering whiff of his aftershave.

Was this how it was for her mam? This jittery feeling? Was that why she gave her dad hell all the time? For a moment, though she knew she'd never be jealous like her mam, *ever*, she thought she understood how she felt.

Chapter 4

Shirley wasn't on her own for very long. Before Keith had even left the dance-hall, two girls around her own age came straight over to say hello to her, introducing themselves as Doreen and Joan. 'Your fella gone to the Red Lion?' Doreen asked. 'Ours as well. So you can stand here with us if you like. Help us fend off the chancers,' she added, nodding towards the lads who hadn't gone to the pub, and were apparently hoping to take advantage of the mass exodus by trying to impress all the now unchaperoned girls.

The other girl, Joan, who had hair bleached almost as white as Shirley's ankle socks, rolled her eyes as the last of the lads going to the pub had filed out. 'If my Paddy comes back in and catches those idiots checking us out, he'll go mad,' she said, pointing to a group of cocky-looking lads who were now staring at the three of them, bold as brass.

'You should be flattered, Joan,' Doreen said. 'My bloody Kenny wouldn't notice someone trying it on with me if we were having it off in the middle of the bloody dance-floor!'

Shirley was shocked at her being so graphic, but it was certainly an ice-breaker, and within minutes she felt she'd made two lovely friends; there was something so appealing about being with the sort of girls who said it like it was, rather than being all stuffy and buttoned up. And, between them, they fended off two or three hopeful advances – well, bar one lad with an enormous quiff, who seemed determined to keep chatting Shirley up, much to the amusement of the others.

'Leave the lass alone,' Joan kept telling him. 'She's taken!'

'A new face,' Doreen whispered. 'And I'll bet he's been clocking you since you got here.'

'I'm hardly that,' Shirley said. 'I've been coming here for ages!'

'No, *him*,' she corrected. 'Which he must be, to be so stupid.' She raised her voice then, and looked pointedly at the lad. 'If he wasn't, he'd know better than to make a pass at Tucker Hudson's girl.'

Shirley grinned, but the lad's face suddenly fell. He might not have known who Keith was – he'd been away in the army, after all – but he obviously knew the name Hudson. And would doubtless have left her in peace at that moment, except he wasn't going to be allowed to.

'Here's your Keith,' Doreen observed, looking beyond Shirley.

'And here comes trouble,' Joan added. Shirley spun around. He was striding across the dance-floor, taking in the scene – she could almost see his mind working – and looking rather more animated – or rather, tanked up – than he had when he'd left.

It had been more like twenty minutes rather than ten, but he'd come back alone, his mates having obviously decided to linger in the pub. Shirley thought fleetingly that she was pleased he'd taken his leave of them to rejoin her, but any pleasure in that was soon taken away by the realisation that he'd veered off from his route to where the girls stood and was walking towards the lad, who was now heading back to his mates.

The girls watched as he stopped dead in front of the group of lads. 'Shit!' Shirley said, feeling a ripple of anxiety in her gut.

'He saw, didn't he? And he's going to say something to that lad, isn't he?' She took in the scene. 'Oh God, and he's on his own. And there's bloody three of them.'

'Uh-huh,' Doreen said sagely. 'Looks like it.'

'Say something, Dor?' Joan said. 'He's a Hudson, remember. I doubt he'll waste energy on small talk. No, he'll nut him, most probably,' she finished, sucking the last of her milkshake up her straw. 'Looks like it might be a lively kind of night after all.'

'But there's *three* of them!' Shirley squeaked. 'Why would he –'

At which point, Keith did. Just as her brand new friend Joan had predicted, he landed a body-bending punch into the hapless lad's chest then followed it up with the promised head-butt for good measure.

She banged her own milkshake glass onto the bar and ran towards them.

'*Keith*!' she yelled anxiously. What on earth was he thinking? There were *three* of them! And even as she screeched at him, they were all jumping in.

Not that it seemed to dampen Keith's enthusiasm for defending her honour. 'You think you can chat up my bird, do you?' he screamed at the boy, simultaneously ducking from the blows raining down and launching straight back in with his fists. But however fearless he was, he was surely no match for three of them, and Shirley decided she'd better get stuck in as well, by trying to grab the smallest of the three of them. He shook her off as if she'd been no more than a gust of wind on his back, though, and as Keith saw her stagger backwards, it only served to rile him more. Back in he went, blood pouring freely from his nose now, kicking and punching past any resistance, and beginning – incredibly – to get the upper hand, as well.

And then Bert arrived to break the fight up. Keith saw him, too. 'You want a go as well, Bert?' he growled, 'go ahead and be my frigging guest, pal.' He raised his fists just as three men in suits grabbed him from behind. Bert grinned – *he's actually enjoying himself*, Shirley realised – as, while two of the men quickly and surely grabbed Keith's arms, Bert and the third man grabbed his feet. Between them, as the three other lads stood back to inspect their bruises, they lifted him off the floor.

'Let him go, you bleeding bullies!' Shirley yelled, tears springing in her eyes, but as she raised her fists to pummel the back of the nearest of Bert's henchmen, Keith spun himself around somehow, twisting his neck so he was facing her.

'I'm all right, Shirl,' he reassured her, winking at her as if in endorsement. 'I'll meet you at the other end of the car park, okay?'

She could only look on, stunned and shaken, as they carried him by his wrists and ankles to the double doors that led to the car park, looking for all the world as if they were giving him the bumps for his birthday.

Oh, God! she thought anxiously. He wasn't about to get a beating, was he? The thought galvanised her and, with a weak smile at her new friends, Joan and Doreen, she hurried after them, just in time to experience another shocking moment as they swung Keith back in unison before launching him straight across the car park.

They were all laughing, as well, which made her furious. 'You bad *bastards*!' she screamed, elbowing them out of the way. 'You could have killed him!' But by the time she'd run across to him, he was (miraculously, it seemed to Shirley) already getting back up again. He must be like a cat, she decided, as he sprung to his feet, engineered to always land the right way up.

Julie Shaw

He began dusting himself down. Muck and gravel stuck to him like a new suit. 'Are you all right?' she asked anxiously, wincing at the blood smeared on his face.

'Me?' he asked, as if it was a completely unexpected question. 'Course I am, love. I'm used to that from them pillocks. Don't you worry, Shirl. Wait till I see them one by one, though.' He grinned. 'Trust me, they won't be laughing then.'

Shirley certainly wasn't laughing now. Did he mean the lads, or Bert's hard men? Either way, was he totally insane? He was certainly fearless, she conceded as he brushed the last of the dust from his lapels. 'Keith, you're still *bleeding*,' she told him, anxious anew. Had they broken his nose? Would he end up with it all bent and lumpy like his mate Titch's? It was definitely still oozing blood. It was beginning to get dark now, and she could see it glistening by the light of the car-park security lamp.

He pressed the back of his hand to his nose and then held it away from him, tutting, before pushing a hand inside the sleeve of his other arm and tugging down a length of jacket sleeve that had obviously been tucked up inside. That done, he carefully wiped his nose with it, before tucking the sleeve carefully up again. The jacket, she realised, had cuffs that matched the collar. Or would have, had the sleeves not been six inches too long.

'What?' Keith was asking her, and she realised she was standing there, gawping. And, transfixed as she was by the bizarre thing she'd just witnessed, she didn't know quite what to say. There was something so singular about what he'd just done that all her anxiety melted away. Instead, she found herself collapsing into a fit of giggles.

Keith stared at her for a moment, just like Titch had earlier, as if she was mad. 'What's so frigging funny?' he wanted to know.

'Oh, Keith,' Shirley spluttered, 'you should have seen your face! When those men got you, and it was just when you were going to hit that lad, and then you were, like, so surprised – so, like, "What's going on here?" and next minute you were up in the air, and … oh my God, I'm going to wee myself if I'm not careful …'

She crossed her legs, tears of laughter spilling onto her cheeks now. What had happened here? By rights she should be sickened and terrified. And here she was laughing like a drain. What had *happened* here? It was the funniest, yet oddest night of her life, and she didn't think she'd ever felt quite so alive.

Keith grabbed her arm, placed it over his, pulled her close against him, linked their fingers, and she felt the same thrill she'd felt earlier on. 'Come on, you bleeding nutter,' he said, glancing down at her watch. 'Look at the time. Let's get you home before that dad of yours sets his firing squad on me, shall we? I can't be doing with bullet holes in this friggin' jacket as well. It's not even mine, I borrowed it off our Annie's husband.'

Shirley glanced at her watch too. It wasn't even much past nine yet.

'But what about your friends?' she asked.

'Oh, I dare say they're still in the pub. Besides, I didn't come out with them, did I? I came out with *you*.'

His gaze met hers then and she thought she might melt from the heat in it. 'But we're all right for time,' she said, as they left the car park. 'We don't have to hurry.'

He squeezed her hand and smiled at her. 'Yeah,' he said softly. 'I know that as well.'

When they reached Shirley's road, her dad was standing on the doorstep, just as he'd promised, one hand in his pocket, the other curled around something that glinted metallically in the moonlight. There was no sign of her mam – probably keeping well out of his way. She groaned. 'Oh, God, he's only bloody standing there with his alarm clock!' she said. '*Honestly!*'

'Here we are, Mr Read,' Keith called to him. 'Safe and sound and home on time.' He slowed and stopped then, still a few doors from hers. 'I better leave you here, love,' he whispered, his breath tickling her neck. 'If he sees the state of me he'll probably have a fit, won't he?'

'Only bloody just, lad, only bloody just!' her father boomed in response, and Shirley decided that he wasn't a pussycat at all. Just the most excruciatingly embarrassing father in the entire world, bar none.

'Leave it, Dad,' she said, slipping past him as Keith disappeared into the shadows. She hurried up the stairs so as not to disturb the feeling that had enveloped her, giving her dad no chance to puncture the bubble of happiness inside her chest.

How long had they lingered? Had it been two minutes or ten? She'd completely lost track, save to know that it had been long enough. Plenty long enough to ensure she had the sweetest dreams tonight. Plenty long enough know that her mind was made up. She took off her cardigan, pressing it against her face, catching a hint of the scent of him. She'd have to tame him, no doubt about it. *Oh, bo*y, as Buddy Holly might have said, she would definitely have to tame him. But that was fine, she thought, touching a finger to her lips, remembering his.

She couldn't wait to get started.

Chapter 5

Shirley clapped her hands over her ears, but it was no good. She could still hear them. So she went across to her record player and turned the volume to ten. But that was no good either. Elvis did his best, being the teddy bear he was, but the sound was still floating up the stairs, even so.

It was Saturday tea-time, and as per usual, her dad had been up in the village for a few pints with his friends. Which always led to the same result as soon as he got home – the 100-question routine from her mam the minute he'd walk through the door. Who had he been sat with? Which 'sluts' were in the Albion drinking without their husbands? Did any of them remind him of the geisha girls he must have been with during the war?

It was relentless and Shirley was fed up to the back teeth with it, so though she'd been happily downstairs, helping her mam bake some cakes, she had no choice but to take herself off up to her bedroom and leave them to murder each other with words till the time came to go to meet Keith.

She lay on her bed and tried to tune her mind back to the music, thinking both about what it must be like to have Elvis Presley singing to you personally and how it had felt when Keith had done exactly that. But it was difficult and was steadily becoming almost impossible; was she imagining it or was the row getting even louder than usual?

It seemed to be, and when she heard her own name keep coming up in the mix, she gave up trying to enjoy a 'peaceful'

Saturday afternoon to find out what they were arguing about instead.

She sat up then went over to take the stylus from the record, and as she did so she heard a smash from downstairs. They were in the 'breaking crockery' stage now, then, which meant they must be in the kitchen. She padded out onto the landing, where she could now hear them plain as day.

And it seemed she'd come to listen at the perfect moment. 'She's the talk of the bloody Albion!' she could hear her dad yelling. 'Gallivanting over to that scummy estate to see *him*! Him whose family are the scum of the earth, Mary! Everyone knows it! They're a bad lot – a *bad* lot, and no good will come of this. What with one brother in and out of borstal all the time' – she heard the scrape of a chair being moved, then her mother shouting, 'So you keep bleeding telling me!', then her dad again, ranting on in the same tone – 'and another one a bloody jailbird. And where does he make his money? Out of gambling and mucky women, that's how! And let's not forget he's also a *murderer*!' the chair moved again, and she hoped her dad was sitting on it, not about to throw it. 'Is that what you want for our daughter, Mary? *Is* it?'

There was a silence – doubtless temporary – and Shirley gripped the newel post at the top of the stairs, trying to take in what she'd just heard. What on earth was her dad talking about? A murderer?

It had been three weeks now – well, more accurately three weeks, six days and twenty-one hours, since Shirley had been on her first date with Keith. Three weeks in which she'd had her eyes opened to what she'd only ever heard and seen in the movies before, her heart feeling like it was turning somersaults inside her chest whenever she thought about him, the flutter in her tummy when he smiled at her and, as of three days ago, something else, too – to how the 'other half' lived.

Shirley didn't really look at it like that, even if her snob of a father did, but there was no question that Keith's background was very different from hers. Shirley knew she was well off compared with most of her friends, and always had been – she was bound to be, after all; with both her parents working and her an only child they never had to worry about where the next penny was coming from.

She knew that – knew the difference between her life and Anita's, but going with Keith to his parents' house on the Canterbury estate had been like nothing she'd seen before. It had almost been like entering another world.

Keith had met her in town at lunchtime and they'd gone to see Clark Gable in a film called *Band of Angels*, which was currently showing at the Odeon. Shirley loved the cinema and she particularly loved Clark Gable, who'd always reminded her of her dad. Keith had treated her, as well. He'd just got a new job at Fox's dyers on Manchester Road and now he was getting a regular wage, he said he wanted to spend it on her.

'Oh, that was so lovely, Keith,' Shirley said when they emerged, blinking, into the brightness of the July afternoon. 'And *so* romantic. I'm so pleased Sidney Poitier helped them both escape so they could be in love for ever.' She sighed contentedly as she slipped her hand into his as they walked. He squeezed it, then led them diagonally across the road – not the way to walk her back to Clayton, as she'd expected.

Shirley was confused. Keith was going out with his mates tonight to celebrate his new job, hence them going to the matinee performance. Hence him then taking her home.

'Oh,' she said, surprised. 'Where we off to? Aren't you taking me back, then?'

'Not just yet,' he said. 'I thought it was time I took you home to meet the family. Mam said she'd do us a pot of tea and some bread and dripping.' He turned towards her. 'If you want to, that is. Just for a bit. Nothing formal. Then I'll walk you back before I meet the lads.'

'That'll be nice,' Shirley said politely. 'Yes, I'd like that.' Though the truth was that as soon as the words were out of his mouth, she felt nervous as hell. What if they didn't like her? What if they thought she was stuck up? What if they took the mick out of her like his sister Annie had? What if – she blanched at the thought – Annie was actually *there*?

'They're going to love you,' Keith reassured her, as if reading her mind. 'Though I'm not sure a posh bird like you is going to love *them*,' he added, bursting out laughing as he ducked to avoid the slap that came winging his way.

The Hudsons lived on a road called Tamar Street, in the middle of the sprawling Canterbury estate. Shirley hadn't been here before, but she knew all about it. Everybody in Bradford knew all about the Canterbury estate. According to her mam and dad, the people who lived there were as hard as they came and didn't give a bugger about anything.

Actually walking through it was another eye opener. It was even bigger than she'd imagined – almost like a whole town in itself – and with her only ever having lived in a village before, it seemed a lot scarier, too. By the time they got to Keith's street she was so nervous about her surroundings that she was seriously regretting having agreed to come. What would the sort of people who lived here think of *her*?

Shirley remembered meeting John Arnold's mum and dad back when she'd first started seeing him and the butterflies that had danced in her stomach then. They were all taking flight again today, only more so. *Stop being silly*, she kept telling herself. *You're almost 18 now. A grown woman!* But the closer they got and the more the contrast between her life and theirs became obvious, the more her stomach lurched at what Keith's family would make of her.

The first thing that struck her was the enormous front garden, though 'garden' was probably the wrong word. The word 'garden' meant something very different from what she saw now. Her own front garden was a fenced area in front of their house, neat and trim, with emerald grass that her father mowed religiously every Sunday.

This front garden looked nothing like that. It was huge, for one thing, and it was also a state – there was no other word for it. The grass was overgrown – in fact, there *was* no grass in places, just patches of dried mud, cracked and crazed from the sun. It was littered with broken bike wheels and various planks of wood, and at the bottom, by the fence, was an old bomb shelter.

'The big houses all had one,' Keith explained, as they walked up the concrete path. 'They built one on each street so that during the war all the families on each street could use them when there were air raids.'

Shirley had never seen a proper air-raid shelter before. She could barely remember the air raids themselves, but her mam had told her that when the sirens went they used to go down Granny Wiggins's cellar, so this was something completely new to her.

'What's down there now?' she asked Keith, wondering about the doubtless dank, spidery darkness of it.

'Probably a load of old junk,' Keith said. 'All us kids have played in it over the years. Our Joe and David had it as their den last, so God knows what they had stashed down there.'

They reached the front door, which, from the remaining strips of paint still gamely clinging to it, was a glossy black a long time ago. Keith squeezed her hand again. 'Don't be shy, Shirl,' he told her. 'And don't expect too much, either,' he added, as he pushed the door open and pulled her into the hallway. It was the first time she'd had a sense that he might be self-conscious about where he lived, and it immediately made her love him even more.

Once inside, the first thing that hit Shirley was the noise. The small hallway led to stairs and a couple of doorways, the first of which Keith now pushed open. The volume, already loud, was now almost ear-splitting, as her eyes took in what looked like about 20 different people, young and old, tall and short, and all seemingly talking at once.

It couldn't be 20, *surely*, Shirley thought distractedly as she hovered behind Keith in the doorway. But it was certainly more people than she'd ever seen gathered in *anyone's* room. There were adults of all ages – some holding babies – kids and teenagers – she could hardly take everything in. And in the middle of it all, sat a man – must be Keith's father, she reckoned – who'd lowered the newspaper he'd been reading, presumably to get a look at the visitor.

Shirley smiled at him politely, and though he didn't smile back, she would have said hello to him as well, were it not for the fact that almost as soon as their eyes had met, he rattled his paper and retreated behind it again.

'Mam!' Keith called across the room to an older woman who was stirring a pot on a big cooking range. 'This is Shirley. I've fetched her for a cuppa if there's one going.' He then turned to Shirley and stepped aside so she had nowhere to hide. As she'd expected, everyone suddenly seemed to notice her. 'This is my mam,' he told her. 'Annie. And that grump in the armchair over there's my dad, Reggie. Come on,' he said, tugging on her hand. 'I'll find us somewhere to sit.'

The room went from the front of the house all the way to the back, and was divided into a front half, which seemed to be for sitting, and a back half, which housed a dining table and was presumably where they gathered to eat. But how on earth did so many manage to get round it? She followed Keith into the back, then looked on nervously as he poked two young lads who were sitting in chairs at the table. 'Shift it, you two,' he barked, grabbing the closest by his shoulder. 'Me and Shirley want to sit down.'

So that must be it. They didn't. They took turns. The two boys, who Shirley judged must be his younger teenage brothers, certainly stood up without complaint and relocated to the floor, where they looked Shirley up and down curiously. She heard a female voice from behind her then. 'That's our Joe and David. They're the youngest of the clan.'

She turned around. It was Keith's sister, Annie, who'd obviously walked in from the back garden – the door was still open – and looked completely different from how she had before. For starters, she had a toddler perched on her hip and a young girl clinging to her arm, who looked about four.

She looked different. She had rollers in her hair, which was covered by a headscarf, but even so, with her painted eyebrows and ruby red lips, she still managed to look stunning. 'I wondered when he'd bring you home to meet Punch and Judy and the rest of us,' she said, grinning at Shirley as she set the little boy down on the floor.

Shirley found herself unexpectedly pleased to see her. And to see her so friendly and welcoming, rather than spiky and sarcastic. In any event, her presence immediately made Shirley feel much less ill at ease. She sat down at the seat Keith was now holding out for her at the table and found herself looking straight at the news. She blinked. Instead of a lacy tablecloth like the one they had at home, the Hudsons' table was neatly covered in the pages of old newspaper.

'Cheeky mare!' Keith's mum was saying, reaching to clip her daughter round the head. 'I'll give you Punch and bloody Judy! Here you are, Keith – two pots o' tea for you and Shirley. Do you want any stew?'

Annie pulled out another chair and joined them both at the table, while Shirley looked in wonderment at what Keith's mam seemed to be handing to him. It looked for all the world like a couple of jam jars. 'So you two finally got round to it, then?' Annie said, as she lit a cigarette and addressed the children. 'Go on, you two, back outside for another run round before we go home. Go on, hoppit!'

Shirley smiled shyly back at Annie. 'We did,' she confirmed.

'Pack it in, sis,' Keith said, taking the tea from his mam. 'Don't show poor Shirley up.'

Shirley looked down at what he'd placed before her. She'd been right. They were actually jam jars full of tea.

'And no thanks,' Keith told his mam. 'We're not staying long. Shirley, do you want some bread and dripping, though?'

Shirley caught the gazes of the two boys who were still on the floor looking at her, feeling as if every eye in the room was on her now. It was only now that she really took in just how many people were crammed in there, including another older man who she thought she recognised at the far end of the room, on the sofa, also reading a paper. Would that be the famous (or, rather, infamous) Charlie? And the young woman, the spit of Keith, this one, except for her platinum blonde hair, also with a toddler on her hip. Shirley racked her brains, trying to recall all the names Keith had told her. So this must be his

sister June. She looked far too young to be either Margaret or
– what was the other one's name? That was it. Eunice.

She returned all their smiles, then looked helplessly at her
jam jar of hot tea. Where did she start? She wasn't even sure
how she'd pick it up without burning herself. Did everyone in
the family have asbestos hands? She remembered Keith's question. 'No, thanks,' she said, suddenly struck by the poverty she
was seeing. 'This is just fine,' she added, gesturing to the jam jar
in front of her. 'My mam will have my tea made when I get
home.'

'You *sure*, love?' Keith's mam said. 'It's a long walk back to
Clayton.'

'I'll have hers then,' one of the boys on the floor piped up.
'If you're sure, like,' he added, blushing furiously.

Which was pleasing. So at least she wasn't the most scarlet
cheeked in the room.

Shirley's embarrassment subsided almost immediately, in fact.
Keith introduced everyone; the other girl *was* June and the
quiet one on the sofa did turn out to be Charlie. She'd been
right; she'd recognised him from back when he'd been in court.
Then there was another man who arrived just after they had
– he was apparently Ronnie – with the same seemingly trade-
mark slick of thick inky hair. And after the niceties had been
observed and she'd finally dared to pick her tea up, the room
returned more or less to the way it had been when she'd arrived.

She'd never heard so many people speaking and joking and
laughing all at once, and she soon forgot about feeling sorry for
them about all the things they didn't have – no proper curtains,
no carpets and, as Keith had already told her, no electricity –
and instead she was soon feeling envious of what they *did* have
and what she definitely didn't: such a big happy family, such an

obvious camaraderie, all those little ones, all that lovely hustle and bustle and noise.

The noise, in particular, felt so strange, but in a good way. Apart from at the weekends, when her mam and dad got drunk (which was always horrible), Shirley was used to polite chit chat, order, meals eaten in silence. This was a much more exciting way to live – as far as she was concerned, anyway – and helped make sense of the way Keith was always so confident and easy going, so at one with himself. She couldn't wait to embed herself within it.

That had only been three days ago, but as she listened to her dad ranting on now, saying such shocking and worrying things, Shirley felt at first angry – who was he to pass judgement on such nice people? – but then, as he'd kept on, confused and concerned. What was he talking about? *Was* Keith's brother Charlie really a murderer? Yes, she knew he'd been in a horrible accident and had lost his brother, wife and baby daughter. Everyone she'd ever spoke to knew all about that. But a *murderer*? Did her dad know something she didn't? Something she *should* know? Try as she might, she couldn't believe it could be true.

Chapter 6

Shirley stayed at the top of the stairs until she was sure that her father was back in his regular 'after-ale' position in the front room on the couch. She'd heard little more that she didn't know already; just that her father thought the whole Hudson family were a bunch of malingerers and ne'er-do-wells and that with 'the kind of man that bleeding Charlie Hudson' was, he wanted his own family to have nothing to do with them for fear of being 'tarred with the same bloody brush'.

Pleasingly, Shirley's mam had at least sprung to her defence, pointing out that Charlie was nearer their age than their daughter's and that she couldn't give a fig what brush she got tarred with, and just dare anyone try to say anything to her face. But it was still depressing, not to say distressing, to hear what her dad had said – had he so little faith in his own daughter that he really believed she wasn't capable of knowing right from wrong? Or of being able to know the difference between a good lad and a bad one? She might not have known Keith very long, but she trusted her instincts even if *he* didn't; he *was* a good lad. He was a fine lad, in fact.

And as for his eldest brother, she'd see for herself. She'd seen or heard nothing to make her wary of him and she wasn't about to make judgements about him based on what anyone else had to say – certainly not based on her father's drunken ranting. Yes, he'd looked a little unkempt, but he'd been perfectly polite and friendly. She certainly hadn't got the impression she'd been sitting in the same room as a violent, dangerous killer. No, she'd simply ask Keith when she met up with him later, and in the meantime, now her dad was sleeping it off and the coast was clear, go back downstairs and finish off what she'd been helping her mam with; not least because she had a plan for one of the Victoria sponge cakes that had been cooling on the rack when her dad had rolled in drunk. Hmm, she thought, going back to grab her bag from her bedroom, talk about pots and flipping kettles.

'You all right, Mum?' Shirley asked as she went back into the kitchen. 'Only I could hear you and my dad arguing from upstairs.'

Mary was at the sink, washing up the cake tins and mixing bowls. She turned around, grabbed a tea towel from the hook and shook her head. 'Take no notice, love,' she said. 'He's just drunk, that's all.'

'Yes, and saying things about Keith and his family again. I wish he'd stop it, Mam. It's not fair.'

'I know, love. But you'll just have to ignore him. You know what he's like. He's just looking for an excuse to start something up before me, same as always. Just to put me off the scent. He thinks I'm bloody stupid, he does,' she said, getting into her stride now. 'He'll have been chatting some slut up at the club and will have had a guilty conscience.'

Shirley sighed. Was that *really* what her mam thought? Things never changed. She knew her mam was all wrong about her dad, as well. Her Granny Wiggins had told her once that he hardly dared speak to *anyone* when he was out, for fear of the wrath that would rain down on his head. He didn't even dare speak to his friends if they had their wives with them, her mam was that jealous. But Shirley knew better than to try to make her see reason; she'd only be accused of siding with him and being disloyal. And what her dad was or wasn't up to wasn't the point in any case. This wasn't about him. She was much more concerned at his opposition to her seeing Keith Hudson, at how much it upset and embarrassed her to think he wasn't welcome in her home.

That fact, in particular, made her crosser than ever, especially considering just how very welcome she'd been made in *his*. 'Mam, I'm sure that's not the case,' she said, just the same as she always did. To which her mam replied – just as she always did as well – that she'd bloody swing for him if it turned out it was.

So there was no point it talking about it any further. 'I'll do the drying up, shall I?' Shirley asked her mam instead, holding her hand out for the tea-towel. 'And Mam, you know I'm going back round Keith's again this evening? Well, I was wondering if it would be all right if I took them one of the sponge cakes.'

Her mam paused in wringing out the cloth she was now holding, ready to scrub the floor and wipe down the pantry shelves. With her working all week, there was hardly a Saturday went by without her attacking the kitchen with scalding water and her trusty Vim. 'That's thoughtful of you, pet,' she said, shaking out the cloth and picking the tub up. 'Of course you can. I'm sure it'll be appreciated, too. I imagine it must be hard for Keith's mam to find a minute to herself – let alone bake a cake. Not with having to run around after so many children.'

Looking at the calm and order of her mam's kitchen and recalling the chaotic back room at Keith's, Shirley couldn't either. She said so. 'Though it's not that many kids, not now. I think there's only about five lads living at home now. Though there's all the grandkids – oh, Mam, the little ones are *so* sweet. But they're so poor. And I mean *really* poor. Not like Anita and my other friends – I mean really, *really* poor. They have almost nothing; I doubt she's even got the ingredients to make a cake. They don't even seem to have any proper cups or plates. I feel so sorry for them, I really do.'

Mary grinned. 'You've been spoilt, girl. You don't know you're born. When I was a kid, there were all of us – your Auntie Edna and Auntie June and Uncle David and Uncle Manny – all of us in one room with only half a bloody floor. We were all poor in those days, love – and them with big families were the worst off of all. You live like a princess in comparison.'

A princess in a lonely ivory tower, sometimes, Shirley thought. Yes, her mam had had a tough childhood – especially when her own mam left her dad, taking all four children with her – but at least they had each other growing up. But what she'd seen at the Hudsons had really shocked her. 'Yes, but to not even have *cups* to drink out of – can you imagine that, Mam? Did *you* all drink out of jam jars? Besides, it's 1958 now, not the olden days!'

'Hark at you,' Shirley's mam said, getting down onto her knees to start on the pantry floor. 'Olden days indeed. No, you've had your eyes opened, and that's never a bad thing. So what d'you want me to do? See if I can rustle up a couple of bits of crockery for them? Not that we've many spare,' she added, with a wry smile, 'not with the way I get through them, eh?'

Shirley smiled back at her mam – that was certainly true enough – but then she shook her head. She'd certainly thought of asking, but only fleetingly; she couldn't really imagine doing such a thing – it would seem much too condescending. 'No, of course not,' she said, 'but I thought it would be nice, since I'm visiting again, to bring *something* at least.'

Mary smiled up at her. 'And you're right to,' she said. 'You're a good girl, you are, Shirley. Tell you what, how about you take a quarter of tea as well? Never met a person who wasn't grateful for a quarter of tea. And you'd better get some buttercream made then, hadn't you? And if you're after some of your dad's strawberry jam you'd best get your skates on before the old bugger wakes up.'

'Have you come bearing gifts?' Keith asked hopefully, three-quarters of an hour later, as Shirley turned the corner to their arranged meeting spot and he noticed the cake tin she was carrying. It was an old, metal biscuit tin they'd had for years, with a lovely wintery scene on it, but her mam had told her not to worry about asking for it back.

Keith was wearing yet another jacket that looked as though it had the cuffs tucked into the sleeves, and his wavy hair had been carefully combed up into a perfect quiff. 'It's just a sponge my mam made and a quarter of tea,' Shirley explained.

'Just?' Keith said, taking the tin from her and sticking out an elbow for her to thread her arm through. '*Just?* Oh, me mam's going to love you.'

She hoped she was right. She still felt anxious that her gesture might backfire. That Keith's mum would take offence and think she was being presumptuous. She was more anxious, however, about the things her dad had said and, working on the basis that if she didn't ask she wouldn't know, she decided to pluck up the courage to ask Keith about Charlie.

'Charlie?' Keith asked her. 'What about him?'

'I heard my mam and dad talking,' she said, 'and they mentioned about the car crash. You know – the one when his wife and baby died … and his – um, *your* brother …'

'And his friend,' Keith added. He fell silent for a moment. 'Her name was Betty,' he said eventually. She was lovely.' He fell silent again, scuffing the toes of his shoes into the dust as they crossed the dirt road up Arctic Parade. 'My sister Annie was hurt, too. Her hips and leg. Badly. She was stuck in Pinderfields for ages.'

'I didn't know about that.'

'Months, it was. She wouldn't come to any of the funerals. Anyway,' he said, looking at Shirley curiously, 'what about it?'

There seemed no polite way of asking him what she wanted to ask him. 'Just, well, just that I was wondering what it must be like, you know?' she said. 'You know, feeling you're responsible for such a tragedy. I can't imagine how that must feel. It must have an effect on a person. It must have been … I don't know. I mean, him going to prison and everything … I still remember that day when I saw you in court, you know.'

Keith smiled at her. 'Me an' all. I remember seeing you sitting there with John bloody Arnold. And thinking how he'd done bloody well. Except not quite so much as he thought he had, you making those eyes at me and everything.' He laughed. 'But, yeah, you're right. Course it affected him. It affected all of us. It affected everything. Me mam still goes to Brian's grave, you know, once a month, regular as clockwork. And every Christmas, of course, what with when it happened. And Charlie … well, you've seen him now, haven't you? Ruined him that accident did. Did for him in lots of ways. He's never been the same since it happened. Probably never will be. How could you be? And the worst of it was that it could have happened to anyone, couldn't it? Well, a lot of people, anyway – it was a terrible, filthy night. But there's no telling him that. There's no trying to make him feel better about it. Anyway, like I say, why the interest in our Charlie? Your mam and dad been listening to gossip?' He turned to face her as they walked. 'If so, it's pretty old gossip, Shirl.'

'Sort of,' Shirley admitted. 'It was just something I heard my dad say. I was wondering … is that why he's been in and out of prison all this time?'

'Your dad?' Keith wanted to know now. 'What *did* your dad say, Shirl?'

Shirley felt a warmth spreading upwards from her neck to her face. But there was no avoiding repeating what her dad had said. Not now. 'It was just – did he kill someone, Keith?'

Keith stopped dead on the track. '*Kill* someone? Who told him that?'

'I don't know,' Shirley admitted. 'I just heard him say Charlie had killed someone, and I wondered if, um, well, what with the tragedy and everything …'

'*Killed* someone?' Keith said again. 'Our Charlie? Don't get me wrong – he's no angel. He's a fighter. And a bloody good one, too. But kill someone? Never. That's not Charlie. He might fall foul of the law, but he's a decent man, Shirl. Besides, you've seen him,' he said, 'and if you've heard the gossip you'll know anyway. He's much too busy trying to kill himself!'

He smiled as he said this, but Shirley saw it differently. Poor Keith. Poor Charlie. Poor all of them, really. She couldn't begin to imagine having something like that happen in your family, and in that moment, for a split second, she hated her dad. Hated him for listening to gossip and calling Charlie a murderer when it was just a tragic accident. Hated him for saying such horrible things. Things she'd no business even *thinking* might be true.

* * *

The house on Tamar Street was quieter today, the grandchildren absent, though there was another brother, Reggie, to be introduced to. He was older, the next one down from Charlie, Keith explained, and was sitting with Reggie senior in the front room.

The two boys, Joe and David, were once again at the table, busy tucking into a pile of chips that sat in their wrapper still between them.

'Hello, love,' Keith's mam said, looking up from where she was stationed at her range. 'How are you, then? Fancy a pot o' tea?'

Shirley felt another rush of annoyance that Keith had been extended no such welcome in her home and vowed that, whatever her dad thought about anything to do with the Hudsons, she'd be doing what she liked from here on in. 'Yes, please,' she said shyly, taking the tin back from Keith and crossing the room so she could hand it to Annie. 'And I brought you this,' she said, holding out the cake tin. 'It's just a quarter of tea and a Victoria sandwich my mam made. Just to, well, thank you for having me the other day.'

Annie took the tin from her and opened it, then stared at the contents, eyes wide, a stunned look on her face. Joe and David, too, both of whom had been busy munching and chattering, stopped talking and turned to look their way.

She could feel everyone's eyes on her now, and felt another blush rising, and for a horrible moment though she had got it all wrong – that *Keith* was wrong; that his mam didn't love her at all – that she thought she was being cheeky offering them charity. But then she saw movement out of the corner of her eye and when she turned to see what it was, she saw Keith's dad rising slowly from his armchair.

'Well, now,' he said to Keith grandly, 'this is your Shirley, is it? And what a vision she is.'

Shirley blinked at him. So she hadn't imagined his indifference the other day. He'd not even really registered that she'd been there. But he clearly had now. He smiled and cleared his throat. And as he did so, she also heard a snigger from behind her – Joe or David, perhaps – and she was aware of Keith, just beside her, trying to keep a straight face. But, undeterred, or oblivious, Reggie stepped to one side and gestured expansively to the sagging seat of his chair. 'Welcome to our 'ome, Shirley lass,' he continued, 'and please, take my seat while I make you a nice jar of that lovely tea you've fetched and a slice of that posh cake, eh?'

And so, Shirley went and sat, aware of the gaping jaws of the assembled company, but unaware – at least till Keith told her when he walked her home later – that for his dad to behave in such a way was unheard of. Now she did feel like the princess her mother had called her earlier, sitting in what was clearly a chair no one else ever sat in, while this man, who she'd previously thought was going to be grumpy and unapproachable, bustled his wife out of the way so that he could personally make her tea and serve her the first slice of cake.

To have this attention lavished on her wasn't new – her mam and dad had doted on her all her life – but to see it here was to remind her that what her dad thought was incorrect. The Hudsons might be poor but they weren't different from the Reads. There were just a lot more of them, that was all.

Chapter 7

January 1959

Shirley glanced over her sewing machine at Annie. 'Is it nearly time for a ciggie break, d'you think?' she called across to her, having to shout to be heard over the din. Doris Day had just come on the radio, the cue for a mass sing-along, which meant it would be a good time to slip away for a quick natter.

She'd had reservations when Keith had first suggested Annie ask about a vacancy, but Shirley loved her new job at Sutcliffe's. She'd enjoyed working at Marsilka, sewing up knickers and fancy underwear, but here they sewed skirts and dresses for Marks & Spencer, and it was piecework. Which was good news for Shirley because, being accurate and fast at sewing, she could make a good deal more money than in her last job. Plus it was fun, particularly the singing and general camaraderie, because at Sutcliffe's they listened to the radio all day long – Mr Mitchell, the big boss, said it was good for morale – and she'd also made lots of new friends.

Annie, in particular, had become a close friend herself now, which was how Shirley had landed the job there in the first place; Annie had gone out of her way to sweet talk Mr Mitchell and put in a good word for her. It never ceased to tickle Shirley that when she'd first met Keith's sister she'd been so wary of her – even a little scared of her, looking back.

Not that she didn't still look up to her. Annie was the best fun, and she was a mine of information – information Shirley was keen to learn. It was Annie who'd convinced her, though she'd have never dreamed of doing so at Marsilka, that to help yourself from the scrap bins at the end of your shift wasn't stealing, it was just one of the perks of what was still pretty poorly paid employment, and that the bosses knew and turned a blind eye.

It had certainly seemed as if all the other girls did it. 'How else are any of us going to have any going-out clothes?' Annie had reasoned. And she'd had a point. Since she'd started there, Shirley had made herself all sorts of lovely things. Lovelier than most, in fact, because she had the rare luxury of her mam's sewing machine to run them up on.

'Go on, then,' Annie said now, biting the end off her cotton and rising from her chair. 'We need a break, in any case. Let the twats catch on we're going so fast and they'll lower our rate, just you watch.' She grabbed her Woodbines and matches from the end of her bench and nodded across the room at Joyce, another friend Shirley had made and who she and Keith saw regularly, her boyfriend Jock being one of Keith's mates.

A minute or so later, all three were lighting up in the toilets, Annie with her foot holding the door open slightly so they could still hear the music from the factory floor and would know when Joe Henderson came on.

Having the radio constantly on made the shifts go much more quickly, but the one they'd probably stay on to listen to even if they didn't have to was *Workers' Playtime*, hosted by 'Mr Personality', Wilfred Pickles. The show was an important part of factory life at Sutcliffe's; all the women loved it and invariably sang along to all the songs. Far and away the best part of the week, however, was when the show hosted their weekly talent contest and the pianist Joe Henderson would visit factories up and down the country to seek out the local talent and host the day's show from the factory itself.

'It's on!' Annie said, opening the door a little wider so they could all sing along to the opening jingle, which had become as routine for the workers as the sewing itself.

'*Have a goooo Joe!*' Annie warbled, through a wreath of cigarette smoke. '*Come and have a go! Here's your chance to have some fun and make yourself some dough. So hurry up and join us, don't be shy and don't be slow. Have a gooooo, have a gooooooo!*'

She then drew on her cig and immediately had a coughing fit, which had her doubled up in the toilet doorway, eyes streaming.

'You're mad, you are,' Joyce said.

'But, you know, you're a really good singer, Annie,' Shirley added, having had a sudden thought. 'You know what you should do? You should ask Mr Mitchell if he'd let you write to the radio and see if you could get them to come here. Then we could have our own singing contest, and I bet you you'd win.'

'I might just do that,' Annie said, once she'd recovered her composure and wiped her eyes. 'Though they never would, Shirl. Come up here? Not in a million years.'

Annie had been wrong. Fired up by the idea of imminent fame and fortune using the fabled Hudson voice, she'd been as good as her word and had gone and spoken to Mr Mitchell, and the following Friday he had them all gather for an announcement; *Workers' Playtime* – and the legend that was Joe 'Mr Piano' Henderson himself – would be coming to broadcast the show from Sutcliffe's the following Monday.

The silence that greeted the news – almost unheard of on the factory floor – was so complete it was almost palpable. And it was immediately replaced by a swell of excited chatter as the reality of the coming visit began to properly sink in.

'Now then,' hushed Mr Mitchell, 'pipe down a bit, you lot. I haven't finished yet.' He cleared his throat and twanged his stripy braces against his beer belly. This always made Shirley laugh as her boss was only in his thirties and yet he always seemed to dress like an old man. 'So,' he continued, 'best get your glad rags out of your wardrobes, ladies, because come Monday, Joe Henderson will be here standing in judgement at the first official Sutcliffe's Beauty Contest!'

'A beauty contest?' Shirley whispered to Annie. 'But I thought it was going to be one for singing?'

'So did I!' hissed Annie. 'That's bleeding typical, that is!'

Mr Mitchell was still pontificating grandly from his pulpit, in reality a self-made platform he used to address the workers composed of a small pile of old pallets. And going on about it as if it had been *his* idea, rather than theirs, Shirley thought. 'Good luck one and all,' he was saying expansively, sweeping both his gaze and his arms in a wide arc around the factory floor. 'And make sure you all come in suitably glammed up for the occasion. Don't be showing us up, now, because it will probably go in the paper as well, and I want us to make a decent splash.'

'Hark at him! Glammed up, indeed,' Annie muttered, giving her boss a dirty look. 'I *knew* he'd do that. I should have realised – he almost said as much when I went in to ask him. Started going on about how it wouldn't be fair as not everyone could sing ...'

'Like me, for instance,' said Shirley, finding she was beginning to warm to the idea now. Not that she *couldn't* sing. She just didn't have Annie's confidence about doing so in front of an audience. Like Keith, Annie would get up on stage at the drop of a hat, whereas Shirley knew she'd be quaking in her boots. But Annie didn't seem to see it in quite the same way that Shirley was. 'Like everyone's beautiful enough to win a beauty pageant, are they?' she wanted to know. 'I told him that an' all. Look around you – half the women here are right ugly bleeders, aren't they? Can't help it, grant you, but still ...'

'Oh, Annie, you didn't actually *say* that to him, did you?'

'Course I did? Why shouldn't I? It's true!'

'Oh, Annie, you *didn't*!' Shirley said again, open-mouthed. 'You can't go round saying things like that!' But even as she said so she knew it was probably true. Annie had a knack of saying the things other people thought but didn't dare say, and though Shirley would never be quite so catty, she did admire Annie's honesty. She'd never say anything behind your back that she wouldn't say to your face.

'Well, I'm quite pleased,' she admitted. 'Because at least it means I can have a go as well now. Not that I'd ever win or anything – not in a million years. But it'll be nice to get dressed up and take part, at least. And watch you grab the prize anyway, just you watch.'

'Me? Not a chance,' Annie said, batting her lashes and feigning surprise at the very thought.

Morning break saw the girls talking of little else. The canteen was buzzing with excitement. 'I can't quite believe it,' said Joyce as she drew on her cigarette and blew out a stream of smoke. 'The actual Joe "Mr Piano" Henderson, right here, in the flesh. Crikey, I don't know how I'll be able to keep my hands off him, I really don't.'

'He's all right,' Annie conceded, her own cigarette dangling between her lips while she adjusted her stockings. 'All right if you like that sort of thing, I suppose. I prefer a bit of rough, myself.' She stabbed a finger in the direction of one of the supervisors, who was helping herself to a cup of tea from the urn. 'Look at her,' she said, clearly keen to move onto more pressing matters. 'She's got no chance. Not a hope of one. Even though you can see she thinks she has. Too lanky, too many teeth and not enough tits,' she finished, crossing the woman's attributes off on her fingers as if running through a list of cardinal sins.

'How many tits does a girl need to win a beauty show, then, Annie?' Shirley ribbed her. 'Aren't two going to be enough, then? If so, that's us *all* done for. Unless you've got a spare one up your sleeve.'

'You know what I mean,' Annie said. 'I'm just sizing up the competition. Which in this case is none – flat as a pair of fried eggs, hers are. Speaking of which, I'm starving. Let's go and get our cuppa and biscuits, shall we?'

Shirley felt the usual frisson of anxiety as Annie said this, because getting their biscuits didn't necessarily mean paying for them. Shirley fervently wished she *did* have some money in her purse to pay for a couple of biscuits, but she didn't, because much as she loved Keith, he always seemed to be penniless these days, which was beginning to be something of a worry. And that was chiefly due to a penchant for bookies and horse-racing that he seemed to share with his parents and older brothers, which meant she was constantly having to bail him out. She 'lent' him money gladly, for his board and lodgings or so he could have a pint or two with his mates, but she also knew she was going to have to have a word with him about it – and she'd recently promised herself that she would.

The one thing she wished she hadn't done, however, was tell Annie she was hard up, because since then it had almost become obligatory, in the long run-up to payday, to pull the stroke Annie had been at great pains to teach her.

It was another of Annie's scams that apparently weren't scams at all, really – rather, 'perks', to make up for the measly rate of pay offered by the fat cats who drove nice cars and dined out on steak but were too mean to stump up for a few packets of custard creams. In short, using Annie's one-coin-in, four-out approach to putting biscuit money on the plate was something akin to a civic duty. As was making a bit of a mess of various garments through the remainder of that Friday afternoon, it seemed. Whether Mr Mitchell would come to know about it was another matter altogether, but the supervisors found themselves having to reject an unusually high number of pieces, resulting in a similarly high level of material ending up in the rag bin.

'And you shouldn't feel guilty about helping yourself from that, either,' Annie had told Shirley more than once. 'Because that's just another little earner for the bosses, as well.' She explained that the contents of the bin, which was kept by the door to the toilets, were taken regularly by the janitor to sell on for scrap; Sutcliffe's got paid for it as stuffing for cushions and upholstery.

'So it's only fair,' Annie reasoned, 'that it ends up in our handbags. Much the better home for it, don't you think?'

Shirley took this as gospel – much as she took most of what Annie said as gospel – and at the end of the day found herself in the right place at the right time; she was able to skip out of the factory to meet Keith with a lovely length of black crimpolene stuffed up her jumper. No, she wouldn't win the competition – however much Keith kept telling her she might on the way home, bless him – but she didn't care. It was a bit of fun for a work day, getting all dolled up to go to the factory – and with

Joe 'Mr Piano' Henderson coming to visit, for good measure. Though she took care not to dwell *too* much on that part.

As Sutcliffe's was such a big factory, with a large number of employees, news of the beauty contest and the thrill of having *Workers' Playtime* come to visit soon became the talk of the whole area. Every hairdresser with a chair going spare had a queue of women begging for it, all eager to outdo each other with their hair. Shirley, who knew her mam would do a lovely job for her on that front, spent most of hers unpicking the material she'd purloined from the scrap bin and re-fashioning it into a pencil skirt and matching top.

'Aw, you look lovely, pet,' Mary said when she tried it on and did a twirl for her. 'And I'll do your hair for you first thing Monday morning if you like, so it lasts. Make you look like a proper film star. What d'you want? A Sophia Loren?'

'That would be brilliant, Mam,' Shirley said, grateful that one thing she did have was a decent head of hair.

'And you'll look the bee's knees with it too, because you've got the bone structure. Bun up on top, couple of wispy tendrils, good spray of my lacquer. You know what? I think you might even win.'

Shirley shrugged. 'I'm really not bothered if I don't, Mam. It'll just make a nice change from going to work in my pinny.'

Raymond, who had seen the fashion show but refrained from passing comment up to this point, now emitted a low grunt from his armchair and picked up his newspaper. Shirley winked at her mam. 'You know, Dad,' she said, 'sometimes you really remind me of Reggie Hudson. He's a lot like you, in many ways, is Keith's dad.'

'I don't bloody think so, young lady,' Raymond huffed from behind his paper. 'And if you ask me, that bloody frock is far too old for you as well.'

'Well, nobody did ask you, Raymond, did they?' Mary snapped immediately. 'So you can shut up and read your paper, you maungy old bugger. She looks bloody beautiful, and you should be proud of her!'

'It's all right, Mam,' Shirley soothed, not wishing to be the catalyst that set off one of their volcanic arguments. 'He says that but it's just talk. I can tell he likes it really.'

The paper rustled again, but there was no brusque rejoinder. Good, Shirley thought. Time to quit while she was ahead and go and finish off her beauty-contest outfit.

For the first time in as long as she could remember since she'd started going to work, Shirley was tickled to find that Monday couldn't come soon enough. And though she'd chosen her lipstick and eye shadow carefully and borrowed her mam's best pearl earrings, she was still under no illusions that she was going to be the belle of the ball. And that was fine. She was just as excited at the prospect of Annie winning it, and of having a whole proper radio show coming from their factory – one that would be heard by people the length and breadth of Britain.

In fact, it felt more like the end of term at school than going to work. There wasn't a woman in the factory who'd not dressed herself up to the nines – even the older ones who didn't want to enter the contest, and who were now busy helping titivate the ones who had. And though Shirley had had the jitters when clocking in (what if she *did* win, and had to go up and collect her prize?) they were soon dispatched by the sheer sense of fun in the air. Not that it wasn't competitive as well – far from it. Every time the clocking-in machine buzzed to herald the arrival of someone new, every head turned to see who it was and what they were wearing, and the air was full of appreciative 'oohs' and 'ahhs'.

Annie, predictably, was looking a million dollars and, as she hurried over, Shirley wondered if she'd manage to look as glamorous when she was 26 and had a couple of little ones in tow.

'No work this morning,' Annie grinned. 'Got that straight from the horse's mouth. Though we'd better make the most of it – business as usual soon as it's over.' She looked Shirley up and down then, 'Shirl, you look *gorgeous!*'

'Not as gorgeous as you do,' Shirley said, blushing at the sincerity in her friend's voice. 'And you, too,' she added, as Joyce came to join them. 'Come on, let's go for a cig in the toilets, shall we? I need to check my hair's still holding up.'

Annie patted Shirley's bun. 'Thought so,' she said. 'You could hold up the bleeding Empire State Building with the amount of spray you've got on that.'

There was a full-length mirror on the toilet wall and it had never been in such demand. There were at least 15 other girls jostling for space.

'Budge up, ladies!' Annie shouted as she carved a path to it. 'The ugly sisters have had long enough now. Time for Cinderella to get a look in. Go on, shift it.'

The crowd soon dispersed and Shirley was, as ever, slightly in awe at how this tiny little woman seemed to command so much respect.

'Annie, you're awful,' she said, as she touched up her lipstick.

'And you're bleeding simple, Shirl!' Annie replied 'We'd have been standing there all frigging day if it was left up to you. You need to stand up for yourself a bit more,' she said, 'she does, doesn't she, Joyce?' She then inspected her teeth and, finally satisfied she was looking her usual sparkling best, clapped her hands together as if in prayer. 'Shirley Read, you still have much to learn, my child.'

Shirley thought she'd learned a great deal already about this exciting new world she was now inhabiting. She'd taken up proper smoking, which had given her access to the gossip in the toilets, had defied her father by continuing to go out with Keith Hudson, and she'd learned the rules about biscuits and scraps and how things at work *worked*. And now she'd learned something else – that when you were actually known as one of the Hudsons, even by association, then the world was a very rosy place indeed.

Having a radio show coming to visit was a new thing for Sutcliffe's, and over the weekend the warehouse staff had been in to rearrange the factory floor for the occasion. The usual pile of pallets, bins of fabric and the sewing machines themselves had all been moved towards the back so that the women could parade in a line to be inspected by the judges. The show had obviously arrived early that morning to prepare for the live show at ten o'clock. Wilfred Pickles himself wasn't there – he stayed at the studios, apparently, but what *was* there, and which took all the women by surprise, was an enormous black piano.

'Blimey,' Annie observed as they entered the sewing room, 'that must have taken some bleeding carting in!'

Shirley's eyes, however, were immediately drawn to the three men who were currently fiddling with a load of wires and leads, and the big muffled microphones that she knew radio people used. One of them was Joe 'Mr Piano' Henderson himself.

Joyce had been right, Shirley decided. He *was* different in the flesh. She guessed he was in his early forties and although he had good hair and a strong jaw, he was definitely not as good looking as she'd imagined. But there was something about him that still oozed celebrity, and though he wasn't really her type any more than he was Annie's, having someone so famous mere feet away from her set her nerves, already twitched, jangling anew. It was hard to keep your eyes off him – and no one bothered trying; there was something magnetic about the way he spoke and the way he looked, and when he got the girls to sing along to his 'Have a go' tune with him, Shirley decided he had the biggest, whitest teeth she'd ever seen in her life.

Time was of the essence, though, so there was no opportunity for swooning; within minutes, the girls were lined up and the contest began, with Annie, since she'd been the one to write in to the BBC in the first place, having the honour of leading the girls on their walk round the factory floor, a picture of elegance in her scarlet pencil skirt and vertiginous heels.

Shirley was struggling a little to walk in her own high-heeled slingbacks, but Annie, that much older and that much more experienced at the art, strutted effortlessly past the judges, hips wiggling seductively, throwing in a cheeky wink for good measure. She was without a doubt the most glamorous, even if not quite a vision of natural beauty, and Shirley felt sure she'd be the one whose name was called.

And so did Annie – you could tell by the grin on her face as the 24 girls who'd entered gathered at the back of the factory, while the judges went into a huddle to make their decision. Joyce thought so too, and so did several of the girls – a couple even said so – and Shirley, whose nerves had settled now it was over, felt it was only now a question of having confirmed what the majority of the girls already knew.

But as Joe Henderson stood up and smiled before clearing his throat, it seemed it wasn't going to be Annie's day. Mr Mitchell had by now joined him up at the front as well, holding an envelope and a huge bouquet of flowers. 'Well done, all of you,' Joe began. 'What a wonderful effort, and I hope you've all had fun today. And I want you to know that you are *all* very beautiful. So, as you can imagine, it was *extremely* hard to pick a winner. But we have now done so, and without further ado I can announce that the winner is …'

Every eye was on him as he strung out the announcement, and Shirley glanced around to see crossed fingers, Annie's included, and some eyes even squeezed shut as they waited in hope. 'The winner *is* …' he said again, before putting them out of their misery. 'Eileen Harris!' he finished, to a round of woops and applause.

'Did he just say Eileen *Harris?*' Shirley whispered to Annie, who was staring, open mouthed, at the judges.

'Bleeding Eileen *Harris?*' Annie repeated, a little too loudly for Shirley's comfort. 'Eileen *Harris?* But she's got bleeding alopecia! What the frig are they? *Blind?*'

The look of shock and disgust on her face was such a picture that Shirley and Joyce couldn't help but burst out laughing, and it was lucky that the cheering drowned the pair of them out, as they were soon both doubled up with mirth.

Not so Annie. '*Look* at her!' she huffed, as the girl strutted up to collect her prize and flowers. 'Look at her! She's got a bald patch as big as a tennis ball on her frigging head! Sneaky cow. Must have hid it from the judges!'

'*Hardly*, Annie,' Shirley said. 'Look – if we can see it, they could.'

'So why'd they pick her, then?' Annie railed. 'How can you win a beauty contest when you've got a frigging hole in your hair? What's the point of calling it a "beauty" contest if it's not?'

'Come on, Annie,' Joyce reasoned. 'She's got a very pretty face.'

'So that makes it *okay*? So if I had an enormous saggy arse, covered in warts, I could *still* win, because it's *behind* me?' she said. 'It's a travesty, that's what it is!'

Shirley thought differently. To her mind, the alopecia was *exactly* why they chose Eileen Harris. To make a point, and perhaps to give the poor girl a bit of badly needed confidence. But she knew better than to mention that to Annie. Not till the dust settled, at least.

True to his word, Mr Mitchell had the girls back at their machines within an hour of the visitors, and their enormous piano, leaving. And fun though it had been getting dolled up for work on a Monday, Shirley rather regretted not having brought in a complete change of clothes, as sitting sewing in her sexy sheath-like skirt and tight top was a very long way from ideal.

There was just the one plus point when, at around three, there was the unexpected pleasure of seeing Keith arrive on the factory floor. Shirley had no idea why – she wasn't due to knock off till five – but even as she wondered what he was doing there at that time, the thought was accompanied by the pleasure of knowing he'd get to see her looking so glamorous.

But it was no more than a couple of seconds before another thought took precedence – exactly why *was* he here? And, more to the point, why were he and Mandy, the supervisor, heading towards Annie rather than her? And why did he look so grey and distressed?

She stopped what she was doing, feeling anxiety grip her stomach, and rose automatically from her machine. Keith was talking to Annie now, and Annie's face had begun to crumple; by the time Shirley had walked around her machine and crossed the space between them, tears were beginning to spill down Annie's cheeks.

'What?' she said to Keith, looking from him to Mandy. 'What on earth's *happened*?'

Keith put an arm around Annie's shoulder and pulled her towards him. 'It's our Ronnie, Shirl,' he said quietly. 'He's dead.'

Chapter 8

Shirley didn't know what to say. All three were now heading up Little Horton Lane and she couldn't think of a single thing she could utter that would make it better. Ronnie had died and there were no words that would help. She felt her age; that was it. She felt too young, too inadequate, too shocked by the notion that a fit not-quite-30-year-old could just lie down and die. But apparently he had. Just closed his eyes and that was that.

Neither Keith nor Annie had spoken in a while now. They just trudged onwards in the bitterly cold wind, both looking down at the pavement, and though Keith held Shirley's hand she felt strangely disconnected from him; it was as if he was in a place where she couldn't yet go.

She wasn't sure she should have come with them, but some instinct had made her, and she was grateful she had her mam's big fur coat pulled around her and for the slippers she'd thought to slip into her bag at the last minute that morning. It suddenly felt like a lifetime ago.

There'd been no discussion about waiting for the next bus. Keith had insisted that waiting was not going to be an option; be it quicker or not (and that would depend if the next bus was on time), Shirley realised that he couldn't stand still. Though, paradoxically, a part of Keith wanted to tarry. He'd already admitted that. 'I'm hoping they'll have taken him away before we get there,' he'd confessed as they set off. 'It was horrible, Shirl, honest. You don't want to see him.'

'I don't know, Keith,' she suggested softly. 'Just to see him one last time?'

His response was just to grip her hand all the tighter.

'But how did it *happen*?' Annie said, breaking the renewed silence that had fallen as they passed St Luke's Hospital, the place where, presumably, Ronnie's body would have been taken or be on its way to. Or would it? Shirley realised there was so much she didn't know. She'd never seen a dead person in her life before. Never even encountered death – not properly, not really. Her Granddad Price had died when she was six but the memory of that was just a blur, and as he'd already left her Granny Wiggins by then, his passing had never really even registered.

'How can you just fall asleep and die, Keith?' Annie was saying now, her breath clouding in front of her. 'People just don't die for no reason. He's not even bleeding 30!'

Keith shrugged his shoulders and hunched his head further into his chest. 'Shut up, Annie,' he said, with surprising sharpness. 'I've told you what I know, haven't I? Just walk.'

Shirley didn't say anything. Just dared to squeeze his hand a little. And was gratified when the action was reciprocated. She felt so sorry for him. Sorry for both of them. Sorry for the whole family. How did you deal with something so wretched? So completely against the natural order of things? She had no idea.

She felt particularly sorry for Annie, and wondered how she might be feeling. It was tragic for everyone, of course, but she felt Annie in particular might be suffering, feeling guilty about having spent half the morning carping on about injustice in the frigging beauty contest; how hollow that felt now. No, *this* was injustice. Not that.

It took a further 15 minutes for them to reach Tamar Street and as they approached the house, Keith slowed and turned to her. 'Me and our Annie will go in first, if you prefer not to, Shirl. You know. See the lie of the land, make sure …' he paused. His face was as grey as the January sky. 'Well, you know. It's not going to be very nice in there, is it?'

Keith nodded towards the house, but Shirley, resolute now, shook her head. No, it wouldn't be very nice; she didn't have the first idea what to do around what would undoubtedly be a shocked and grieving family, but why else had she come? Why else but to comfort Keith, try to be helpful, see what she could do. 'It's okay, Keith,' she said firmly. 'I'll come in with you. I want to.' She felt Annie grip her arm even as the words left her mouth. So she obviously wanted her there anyway. 'I'll stay as long as you want me to, then I'll walk myself home,' she finished. 'Come on,' she added, taking the lead and turning up the path.

The scene as they walked in was like something from the movies, Shirley thought, a glance around her taking in all the elements. Keith's dad was sitting rigid in his chair, his face as grey as Keith's, and looking suddenly, rather scarily, so much older. Their mam was on the couch, her body turned inwards, as if she was trying to disappear into herself, sobbing into a handkerchief while being comforted by their June. Reggie, Keith's second oldest brother, and his wife Vera were there as well. They were sat at the table, talking quietly with Joe and David. There was another lad there as well, standing in the corner of the front room, gazing out of the window, who, from the look of him, seemed part of the family, but Shirley hadn't seen him before. A nephew, perhaps? She tried to work out whose he might conceivably be, before remembering – there was another brother who hadn't been around, wasn't there? Younger than Keith, too, so this lad might just conceivably be him.

'Our Malcolm,' Keith supplied, having obviously noticed her staring. 'Been locked up for a bit. Just got out yesterday,' he added, before going over to sit beside his distraught mam.

Shirley felt marooned then. An island in a sea of distress, and so was very grateful when Vera patted an empty chair beside her at the table and signalled for her to sit. 'The ambulance has just left with Ronnie in it,' she whispered, leaning closer. 'Poor bleeder.' She made the sign of the cross and then reached across to squeeze her husband's hand.

Malcolm crossed the room then, perhaps noticing there was someone different in the midst. He looked to be in his late teens and Shirley quickly recalled all the snippets she'd heard about him from the others; a bright lad, very funny, but if there was trouble around, you could almost guarantee that Malcolm would be in the thick of it.

He was certainly in the thick of it now. 'You must be Shirley,' he said, reaching the table and holding out a scrawny hand. 'I'm Malcolm,' he added. 'The good-looking brother. I've heard a lot about you.'

As introductions went, it was a surprise, given the circumstances, but Shirley could see past the half-smile stuck on his lips to the bewildered teenager underneath. One who didn't know what to do or say any more than she did. Sensing that made her feel a little more like a grown-up. But before she could do more than return such a smile as seemed appropriate, his brother Reggie tutted sharply and tore him off a strip.

'You've heard bugger all,' young Reggie growled as he glared at his brother. 'You've been in the nick for the last six months, you little toe rag. Now go sit down somewhere and show a bit of respect.'

Malcolm walked over to the fireplace and put the pan on to boil, and she wished she could pluck up the courage to go and join him; jump up and bustle about, being useful, making that traditional pot of tea. But she couldn't seem to find the gumption to actually get up and do it. Instead she felt paralysed by self-consciousness, strange and out of place. The grief was palpable; it seemed to hang in the air like a curtain, and the house, usually so loud and raucous, suddenly looked as dismal as the steadily darkening afternoon. The sound of Keith's mum's sobbing was quiet but at the same time deafening, as if it knew it had the right to drown out every other sound.

Shirley looked across at Keith, at his pained, drum-tight face, and noticed how precisely it echoed the whitened knuckles he held clenched around the top edge of the sofa. He was hurting so much and she didn't know what to do or say. She really wished she could take him away somewhere, hold him tight, encourage him to cry.

But the clamouring silence was about to be broken anyway. Just as Shirley was trying to decide whether to just have a quiet word with Keith and slip away, or to go and help Malcolm by the range, the front-room door was flung open and Charlie burst in. He was clearly drunk and he looked dirty and unkempt.

'Where is he?' he yelled. 'What've you done with him? Where's our Ronnie?' He staggered into the room and made a beeline for his mother. 'Mam! Tell me! It's not true, is it? Please tell me it's not true!'

Everyone's head had snapped up at Charlie's entrance and one by one they all seemed to swivel in the same direction – towards their dad, who seemed to be coming out of his trance-like stare. He too looked at Charlie, and Shirley held her breath: she knew enough about enough to know that they didn't get on. She breathed out as quietly as she could, feeling herself shrinking back into her seat, knowing that things might be about to get nasty.

'Sit down, Charlie,' Reggie said, quietly. 'Our Ronnie's died.' Charlie did so, taking up space on the sofa beside his mother, who extended a hand to take hold of his as he did so. Reggie waited a moment before speaking, easing his body forward in the battered armchair. 'The doctor said it was probably something on his brain,' he said slowly. 'From the car crash.'

Charlie stared at his dad for a long time before putting his head in his hands. Then he began to move, rocking slowly back and forth, groaning softly. And, watching him, Shirley felt tears begin to slide down her cheeks. How *did* you get over something so terrible, she thought. *Could* you?

'Don't you dare!' Annie yelled at Reggie, making Shirley jump. 'Don't you *bloody* dare!' She jabbed a finger towards her husband. 'The doctor said no such thing! He didn't, son,' she said, grabbing one of Charlie's hands and cradling it in her own. 'He asked him and the doctor told him nobody could ever know that. So don't you bloody dare!' she shouted again at Reggie senior. 'It was just one of those things,' she said brokenly, putting her arm around Charlie's shoulder. 'He'd been working on the coal all morning, fit as a fiddle. It's no one's fault, Charlie, you hear me, son? No one's.'

Young Annie, looking so strange in her beauty-contest finery in this room, stepped in front of her dad and pointed in his face. 'How could you?' she wanted to know. 'That bleeding crash was over two years back! How could you bring that up now, Dad? How *could* you?'

'You tell me why then!' Keith's dad said, leaping up to his feet. 'Come on! Why'd he die then? Eh? Come *on*!' Shirley flinched, watching him, seeing the raw emotion spilling from his words. 'My lad comes home from the coal, gets his head down on the couch for a bit, and then just dies? Just goes and *dies*? How the bleeding hell does *that* happen?' He sat back heavily into his chair again, tears running freely down his cheeks. 'He asked me to wash his face, Annie,' he sobbed, tears running freely down his cheeks. 'Asked me to wash his bleeding face so he didn't mucky the cushion. I washed the coal dust off his bleeding face and then he *died*!'

Shirley wasn't sure she could stand any more. She felt dreadful in a way that she'd never before felt dreadful. And also gripped by a sudden claustrophobia. She wanted to be anywhere but where she was right now.

'I have to go,' she whispered to Vera. 'I'm sorry, Vee, but I have to go now.' She looked for Keith, who had both arms round his mother and looked so wretched, but still, seeing her, looked concerned – looked as if he was about to stand up.

Shirley shook her head. 'No,' she mouthed. 'No, you stay with your mam, Keith. I'm all right walking. You stay. Let me know if there's anything I can do.'

She glanced at Keith's mum and dad – both were oblivious – and then to Charlie. He was still rocking and groaning and the sound tore right through her. She'd never been so close to death before, and the raw horror of it scoured her emotions. When the cold night air hit her, it was as if it was trying to rip her lungs out of her chest.

She hurried home alone, striding along streets that would once have scared her, but which now held no fear for her at all.

Chapter 9

Shirley knew that good things could come out of bad things, and it seemed to her, by the time Ronnie had been laid to rest a couple of months, that perhaps the good thing was the way it had cemented her relationship with both the lad she loved and the family of which she now felt such a part. In truth, she felt more a part of the notorious Hudson family now than perhaps she did with her own kin over in Clayton.

That was the thing with death, she'd decided, as she stood at Ronnie's funeral service – it made you realise how few things really mattered. They'd probably never know why he died – 'just one of those things', everyone had agreed – but though the unspoken assumption was that it must have been related to the car accident that had killed his brother, since the day of Ronnie's death, Reggie senior hadn't mentioned it again. There was simply no point, and Shirley sensed he knew that. And, in a strange way, given his hostility to Charlie, it made her warm to him.

It had been a horrible day – the first funeral she'd ever been to – and as they assembled in readiness she felt a pang of a real anger at her parents for 'protecting' her, as they saw it, from harsh realities of life such as this.

But as she'd gripped Keith's hand, she knew she had to be strong for him. It didn't matter that the tears were rolling unchecked down her own cheeks. Watching the Hudsons trying to be so brave as they buried one of their own – and one so young – she felt the strongest conviction yet that Keith was the one, and that she would always be there for him, no matter what. If he proposed she knew her answer would be yes.

When that day might come, though, she hadn't the slightest idea. And, more to the point, what her father might say about it. Though he'd been politely sympathetic to news of Ronnie's sudden death, it was yet more grist to the mill that he kept pounding away at; that Charlie Hudson was a bad lot – look at the fresh tragedy he'd visited on them! – and that, by extension, Keith Hudson was probably a bad lot as well.

'Does he *have* to ask my dad, Mam?' Shirley asked Mary, when they were chatting about the prospect of a future wedding one Saturday morning, Shirley having confessed to her mam how she felt.

'Yes, love, you know he does. That's the law, I'm afraid. Well, unless you're 21 – you can do what you like then, whether he likes it or not. But, you know, love, I'm sure he'll be all right about it now. You've been courting nearly a year now, after all.'

Twenty-one? Shirley's heart sank at the prospect of having to wait that long for Keith to propose – she'd practically feel like an old lady! And she didn't share her mother's confidence, either.

'I'm not so sure,' she said, as her mam pulled a batch of scones from the oven. 'He's always trying to find reasons why Keith isn't good enough for me. Spends far too much time down the frigging pub or up at that club listening to gossip.'

Which was the problem that vexed Shirley the most. Because the truth was that if her dad listened to gossip, he'd surely find it – not least because it was fairly common knowledge around and about that Keith was no different from his feckless older brothers and would regularly blow all his wages on gambling. So it was a knocking bet that her dad knew that too. He'd not said as much – she wasn't sure if her mam even knew about it – but Shirley knew he was well aware that to say so would annoy her; no, he'd be keeping it in reserve so he could bring it out if and when Keith *did* propose, and, however much Shirley might wish it not so, he had a perfect right to refuse her hand to a man who couldn't support her financially.

Which made it a priority that Shirley work harder to straighten Keith out, and make sure he had all *his* priorities right before that happy day came dawning.

Starting right now, she decided, as her mam buttered a hot scone for her, because much as she loved all the members of Keith's family, she wanted to marry a man who could support her as well. And that wasn't because she couldn't earn her own money (half the time, currently, it was her supporting *him*) but because she wanted a family, which meant extra mouths to feed, which meant him pulling his weight when it came to bringing a wage in. The last thing she wanted was for him to become a bit of a rogue, like half the Hudson men seemed to have turned out to be – not to mention a drinker like his dad *and* his mam.

She smiled to herself, recognising that, actually, she wanted it all. She wanted him tamed, well behaved and busy making an honest bob, but at the same time the last thing she wanted to happen was for him to turn into a big softie like John Arnold.

She grinned at her mam, wondering what Keith would have to say about it if he could hear what she was thinking. 'Not that he's shown the slightest hint that he's even going to ask me,' she admitted.

Mary rolled her eyes. 'And that's a good thing,' she rebuked her. 'You're doing too much daydreaming, young lady. You've got the rest of your life to worry about being married. And trust me, girl, it's not as bloody rosy as you think it is!'

Not in her mam's case, perhaps, Shirley thought privately. But then she wasn't her mam, was she? And Keith certainly wasn't her dad. No, *her* marriage would be one of love and companionship, not nasty drunken rows every Saturday.

But her mam was probably right, even so. She was still only 18 and before she worried about Keith's proposal, she should first worry about licking him into shape. And there was no time like the present, she decided, as she finished drying up for her mam and went up to her room to get ready. Not least because they were off to the Tudor that afternoon, a café bar in town that played all the latest music and where everyone hung out, but where, in reality, she would spend most of her time with Annie and June and Joyce, while Keith nipped in and out of the Unicorn pub further up town to have a few pints with his brothers.

She picked up her hairbrush and studied her reflection in the mirror, conscious of the frown lines furrowing her forehead. She wasn't sure why – perhaps the knowledge that her dad might have a point? – but as she dragged the brush through her hair, she felt annoyed. Why should she and the girls have to hang around sipping bloody sarsaparillas while the blokes were living it up in the Unicorn? There might be a law about parents having to sign to let their daughters get married, but since when was there a law that said girls couldn't go to the pub their lads were going to? It went further than that, actually, as most of the pubs had tap rooms that only allowed men in them. The fellas would congregate in those elusive, smoke-filled rooms, leaving their women twiddling their thumbs in the lounge or concert rooms – it was stupid in Shirley's opinion. But it was one thing to have separate rooms within the pubs, quite another to leave them out altogether. Why *couldn't* they go along with them? It suddenly seemed ridiculous.

And perhaps the time had come for her to make her feelings known. She grinned at her reflection, imagining Keith's reaction to her putting her foot down about it, smoothing the lines out along with the tangles.

As Keith and Shirley lived in opposite directions from the Tudor, she'd planned to hop on the bus and meet him in there. But when she pushed open the door it soon became apparent that he wasn't there. She scanned the benches that lined the walls, all fronted by their red shiny tables, taking in the familiar groups of young people, all chatting – and probably gossiping – and tapping their feet in time to the music, under walls hung with pictures of the latest pop stars and actors.

There was never an old person in sight and that was exactly why she liked it; no one to tut disapprovingly, or tell them to turn the music down or make some disparaging comment about a song in the hit parade, or the haircut of whoever was her latest crush.

Unfortunately there was no sign of Annie or June either – just Joyce, who was standing by the Wurlitzer, sipping a milk-shake through a straw, and who now raised an arm in greeting. It seemed her Jock was nowhere to be seen either.

'Over here, Shirl,' Joyce called above the din of the chatter and the sound of Bill Haley coming from the juke-box. 'Keith's already got you a drink.'

Shirley joined Joyce at the side of the machine. 'Oh, he has, has he?' she said, taking it from the table where June indicated. 'Where is he then? Pub with your Jock?'

Joyce grinned as she nodded then leaned closer in, putting her lips almost against Shirley's ear. 'I wouldn't be too mad,

Shirl,' she whispered, obviously sensing her irritation. 'Jock told me they've got a right little scam going on. I think we could be in for a few treats later on.'

Shirley sighed as she reached into her handbag for her cigarettes. 'What do you mean, "scam"?' she asked Joyce as she rummaged around to find them. 'Keith had better not be up to no good. What are they doing?'

Joyce placed a hand over hers just as she was about to pull out her packet of ciggies. 'You won't be needing those,' she said, her voice filled with an air of authority. She moved closer still. 'Technically, it's called "selling fresh air", I think, but look …'

She unclipped her own handbag and opened it just enough that she could show Shirley what was inside. Shirley gawped. It was filled with cigarettes – it looked like there were hundreds of them in there. Not in packets, but loose at the bottom. No wonder she was carrying such a ridiculously big bag, Shirley mused, while trying to work out the significance of what she'd just seen. If Jock and Keith had some dodgy money-making thing going on, why the hell was Joyce spending it all on ciggies?

Joyce laughed as she plunged a hand into the jaws of her bag. 'Your face, Shirl! Don't look so worried, it's fine. Here, look.' She scooped a large handful of cigarettes out and opened Shirley's bag so she could stuff them inside. 'You take these. There'll be plenty more where they came from.'

Shirley quickly tried to hide what she was sure were the ill-gotten gains she now had in her bag. She hated anything to do with breaking the law, and having accepted the cigarettes filled her with the usual anxiety. What if someone had seen? She made a point of lighting one of her own cigarettes. 'Look, Joyce,' she said sternly, 'just tell me what the bloody hell is going on. Not to mention where the bloody hell they are!'

'All right! Keep your hair on, Shirl,' Joyce replied, then proceeded to explain precisely what the 'right little scam' was, in suitably hushed tones.

And a 'right little scam' was what it turned out to be. Keith and Jock had apparently clubbed together to buy two sleeves of ten packs of 200 Park Drive cigarettes. They'd then carefully opened eight of the ten packs in each sleeve and removed the cigarettes. They had then filled the empty packets with sawdust, apparently, leaving a real, unopened pack at either end, so that the sleeve not only looked like any other, but felt the correct weight as well.

'And now they've sold them?' Shirley wanted to know, feeling a rising exasperation.

Joyce nodded. 'At five shillings a pack – which is less than half price. So the punters think they're getting a right bargain, and Keith and Jock are on a right little earner,' Joyce continued. 'All that money and all these ciggies, too! Can't go wrong really, can you?'

Shirley wondered about Joyce sometimes. How could she be so naïve? There were so many ways in which it – *they* – could go wrong. Getting nicked being one of them. And having your face filled in by angry punters once they found out they'd been duped being another. 'Anyway, they've been and bought another six sleeves now they've shifted the first two,' Joyce was saying, causing Shirley to roll her eyes in frustration.

'Can't go *wrong*?' she hissed. 'Joyce, it's bloody criminal! You can't do things like that. They'll end up in the clink if someone puts the police onto them!'

Joyce lit one of the cigarettes from her handbag and shrugged. 'Oh, stop worrying,' she soothed. No one'll get onto them. They'll be *fine*. Anyway, you got any change on you?' she asked, turning to the juke-box. 'I fancy a bit of Ritchie Valens. How about you?'

Shirley felt gloom settle on her shoulders. How ironic that she should have been thinking about straightening Keith out today of all days. If her dad found out about this little number he'd have a bloody field day. She fished in her bag again for her purse – better than Joyce bloody opening hers – and as she pulled it out saw the partners in crime themselves strolling in.

Rather than the flutter of attraction she usually felt on seeing Keith, now she responded to his cheery grin with a scowl of anger. *Look at him!* She thought, *as if butter wouldn't melt in his bloody mouth!*

'Fancy a drink, girls?' Jock asked in his drawling Scottish accent as Ritchie Valens started burbling away behind them. Jock was a lovely bloke, actually – always had a bright beaming smile, and was kind with it. He'd do anything for anyone. But today all Shirley could think of was how important it was that she make a stand, which, unfortunately for Jock, meant his charms wouldn't wash.

'What?' she snapped. 'You mean out of the money you've just conned in the pubs? No, thank you, I'll buy my own bleeding drink.' She turned and glared at Keith then, grimly pleased to see the look of surprise on his face. 'In fact, I've just changed my mind,' she said. 'Yes, I *will* have a drink, and so will Joyce. Not in here, though. I think we'll nip into the Unicorn for a glass of bitter.' She turned to Joyce, hoping she could rely on her. 'You ready?'

Keith and Jock stared at each other, both looking decidedly uncomfortable at this unexpected turn of events. 'Er, well, me and Jock *were* just going to nip to the Boy and Barrel for a swift one,' Keith said. 'But we won't be long.'

Shirley grabbed the cardigan she'd only just taken off. 'That's fine. The Boy and Barrel will do equally well,' she said firmly. 'Come on then, Joyce. What's good for the goose is good for the gander, isn't it?'

'But we're only going to be gone ten minutes,' Keith persisted. 'Why don't you two wait here for us, and then we'll all go up Manchester Road for one instead.'

'Why?' Shirley demanded, already making her way to the door, Keith trotting along in her wake. 'In case one of the punters you've scammed has realised he bought sawdust and comes looking for you? Well, if that's what you're bothered about, you deserve a bleeding crack. What is *wrong* with you?'

The penny finally dropping, Keith glared at Joyce as they all walked out onto the cobbled street. 'Big mouth!' he huffed. 'You couldn't keep it shut, could you?'

Shirley jabbed a finger at Keith, secretly pleased that at least he knew full well how much she disapproved. 'And don't you *dare* bleeding blame her, Keith Hudson!' she shouted. 'Why can't you be happy just earning a wage like everybody else, Keith? Instead of always being on the bloody look-out for the next con? What's the matter? Have you blown your wages in the frigging betting office again?'

Did she see a flash of remorse on his face at that point? She certainly hoped so. Though she was genuinely cross with him, she was also well aware that she was overplaying her anger just a little. But then she needed to, didn't she? To press her point home. Because no matter how much she loved Keith, this was a turning point, she realised. The point where Keith would hopefully realise that she wouldn't sit on the sidelines all the time, looking pretty and waiting – always waiting and waiting – while he strutted about Bradford, thinking he could do what he liked.

No, today was going to be different. Taking his continued silence as an admission of guilt, she looked back towards Joyce and Jock, who both still looked stunned.

'Come on then, you two,' she said, 'the Boy and Barrel won't come to us, will it?'

She then gripped Keith's arm and led the procession of four up Ivegate to have the drink she felt she very much deserved. Despite what she'd said to Joyce, she wasn't really worried about any unlucky punters coming after them. Jock was a giant of a man, and Keith was – well, Keith was Keith, wasn't he? One of the Hudsons. Untouchable.

She allowed herself a secret smile and squeezed his arm fondly. No, they'd be fine. But as far as she was concerned, that was *it*. He might think he was moulding her into a suitably tough Hudson woman, with all his ducking and diving and scams and general naughtiness, but he was wrong. She was moulding *him*.

Moulding him into suitable marriage material.

Chapter 10

November 1959

One thing about sitting at the newspaper-covered dining table in the back room at Tamar Street was that there was always something to read. It was warm too, which was welcome after Shirley's chilly walk to Canterbury from Sutcliffe's, the range now crackling away cheerfully just behind her, Keith's dad having stoked the fire as soon as she'd arrived.

It would be Christmas soon and Shirley was determined to do something for the Hudsons. After all, given the amount of time she spent there these days, it only seemed fair. Though Keith had told her they didn't really bother with things like trees or baubles, she'd already decided that, if she could afford to do so, anyway, she was going to pop down to Woolies and get some decorations so that she could contribute something festive to the household.

And she was confident she would be able to afford to, as well. Since she'd persuaded Keith, back in the summer, to let her take charge of at least some of his weekly pay packet, they were a lot better off than they had been. And unless he was very devious (and she didn't think he was) he'd been keeping out of the bookies as well. It wasn't just the money they saved that made Shirley happy, either; it was the fact that he seemed to be making a commitment to being responsible, which was all grist to the mill where talking her dad round about her boyfriend was concerned.

And, oh, how she wished her dad could know the Keith *she* knew. She glanced again at the piece of paper she held in her hand now, before she re-folded it and slipped it back into her handbag. She'd almost missed it – tucked between her purse and her pack of tissues, it wasn't easy to spot, after all. But as soon as she saw Keith's uncommonly beautiful script-like hand-writing – which was now so familiar – she'd known exactly what it was.

The note safely stashed, she picked up her jar of tea and took a sip. As ever, it was strong and scalding, because that was the way Reggie made it, so she went over to the sink to add a half-inch of cold water. 'Are you sure there's nothing else I can do, Reggie?' she called over to where he was sitting in his armchair. 'I could tidy the back room or something if you want, just till Annie gets back. Make myself useful.'

Shirley had already laid the table. It was the first thing she tended to do for Annie when she went round after work for her tea – something she did two or three times a week these days. Her own mam and dad couldn't understand it. The Reads were a meat and two veg kind of family and Mary worried that Shirley wouldn't be getting enough 'nourishment'. Shirley had long given up explaining that when you'd been forced to eat bloody liver and onions and big steaming dinners all your life, egg and chips – or even dripping and bread – were a very welcome change.

So she'd carried on. After all, she was a grown woman now, wasn't she? And, knowing when she was beaten, Mary had stopped nagging her about it. In fact, she'd now got into the habit of baking an extra batch of scones or a Victoria sponge cake, just so Shirley had something to take with her from time to time. 'It's the least I can do,' she'd said when Shirley assured her there was no need. 'It's only right, since they're feeding you so regularly.'

But Shirley had arrived early today, which meant Keith, who still worked at Fox's Dyers, wasn't back yet and, unusually, Reggie was the only one at home. Annie had gone to the chip shop on Central Avenue to get supplies, and Joe, now finished in school, was still out painting somewhere. He'd started a job for Joe Laine, the same decorator that Keith used to work for, and Shirley knew how much the extra pay packet meant. And with only one left in school now – well, most of the time, anyway – things would hopefully get a bit easier for them.

'And our David is out goodness knows where,' Reggie had explained when she'd first arrived. 'Little sod that he is, he's probably out raiding some poor bugger's shed. That's his latest bloody pastime – Keith tell you? He'll end up sharing a bedroom with our Malcolm again if he's not careful, that one will.'

He'd gone to make the tea then, and though Shirley was happy enough, she still felt self-conscious around Reggie when there were just the two of them there, and badly in need of something useful to be getting on with.

'No, love,' Reggie said now, in response to her question, 'you just sup your tea and rest your legs for a bit. It must take you a good 20 minutes to walk up that hill and across here, mustn't it? No, you stay put. Annie won't be long.'

Shirley picked up her tea, which was finally cool enough to handle, and went to sit on the sofa in the front room with him. He grinned at her as she perched on the edge of it. 'And what was that tickling you just now, my girl, anyway? Don't think I didn't see you having a giggle at the table.'

Shirley coloured. She hadn't even realised he'd been taking any notice. 'Oh, nothing,' she said. 'Just a little poem from your Keith, that's all.'

Reggie grinned again at her. 'Thought so,' he said, looking very pleased with himself.

Shirley hoped he didn't want her to read it to him. Keith often wrote her poems that were so funny they made her laugh out loud, and which she could never wait to show her mam, if not her dad. But at other times he popped soppy love letters in her handbag. Soppy enough to make her blush. And this was one such. So she definitely didn't want to share it – not with her mam and definitely not with Reggie.

But it seemed he didn't want to hear it anyway. 'Gets it from me, you know, Shirley,' he said, placing his paper on his lap. 'You know – his way with words. Bit of a family trait, that.'

'I know,' Shirley agreed. 'He's really clever with them, isn't he? Does lovely verse for birthday cards as well.'

Reggie nodded. 'That he does, lass. Chip off the old block is our Keith. Here,' he said, leaning forward in his armchair and clearing his throat, 'I've got one for you – give you a bit of a giggle. *De spring is sprung, de grass is riz, I wonder where de boidies is? Some say de boid is on de wing, but dat's absurd – I've always hoid dat de wing is on de boid!*'

Shirley laughed at his impromptu performance. 'Did you make that up yourself, Reggie?' she said, cupping her tea between her hands to warm them.

He shook his head. 'No, lass, I didn't. Not that one. Don't know who did, truth be told. Not that I didn't pen a few gems of my own, back in the dark ages. Only trouble is, my old brain can't blinking remember any of them.'

'Aww,' Shirley said, smiling at him. 'Did you write poems for Annie?'

Reggie chuckled. 'That I did. Though only for the first year or so. Maybe less than that even,' he added dryly. 'Didn't seem any time at all before nippers and nappies took over our lives.' He paused then, before winking and correcting himself. 'Well, that and the fact that my Annie turned out to be a bleeding lunatic o' course.'

Shirley couldn't help but burst out laughing at that. And her own chuckles made Reggie start laughing as well. It was rare that she ever got to see this side of him and it pleased her; she knew without a doubt that as soon as Annie or one of the others walked in, he'd pick up his paper and immediately resume reading it, further contributions consisting only of occasional grunts from his chair. It was just the way he was, and she accepted this – her own dad, when he had a mind to, being exactly the same.

She glanced out of the window, aware of how quickly the light was fading. Though it was only five o'clock, it was already getting dark outside. The street lights were coming on now, illuminating the estate and, to Shirley's mind, making it look so much nicer than, in reality, it was.

Reggie was watching her. 'Shall I tell you something, Shirl?' he said. 'If you stare through that glass long enough you'll start to see the ghost of Horsewhip Aggie!'

He chuckled again as she dropped the piece of curtaining she'd been holding up and went across to the far side of the window. Horsewhip Aggie was apparently legendary round these parts. A hag of a woman, who was said to have completely lost her mind, she was the sort of character who so fascinated the local kids that, despite their terror of her, they'd still dare one another to torment her by knocking on her door and running away – not least because she'd then come roaring out of the house carrying a big horsewhip and threatening to choke any kid she found with it.

She was long gone, apparently, but her ghost clearly lived on. Being constantly threatened by a visit of the ghost of Horsewhip Aggie was one of the first stories Keith had ever told her. Reggie'd winked but she could imagine him threatening them with her too; it was funny, she thought, how similar her and Keith's parents were, despite having such different lives. They were both stern men who inspired respect and fear in other younger ones – her dad at work, and Reggie in his own lads and among the community generally – but who were both married to women who not only gave as good as they got, but more often than not more than they got as well. She'd not had that much exposure to Annie's rants at Reggie as yet, but Keith had told her enough to know she was a force to be reckoned with, even if not quite the lunatic he'd cheerfully described her as.

She pulled the other piece of curtaining across to shut out the night. It was the week after firework night and the street outside still bore the remnants of the huge bonfire that the residents of the street had, to her bemusement, lit right there in the middle of the road. It was bizarre. And certainly nothing like the plot nights Shirley remembered from her childhood. Back in those days, she and her mam and dad would light a small fire on the field opposite their house and all the neighbours and their children would come along. Everyone would bring something nice to eat as well: fruit, pie and peas, rock-hard homemade treacle toffee that you could suck on for ever, and delicious, nutty potatoes that had been almost burned to a crisp in the bottom of the fire.

Here, though, with no fields at the end of a lane to use, the residents just organised their parties out front. It wasn't just Tamar Street that had a bonfire roaring in the middle of the road, either; there were huge fires dotted all around Canterbury estate, built with enthusiasm by all the neighbours. They'd start in the morning, with people turning up with their 'chumping' throughout the day, building up a pyramid that consisted of anything combustible – planks and offcuts of wood, chairs and armchairs, old toys and tyres; in fact anything that would burn, got burned. And instead of toffee apples and pies, the fare for the occasion was vinegar-soaked chips and as much cider or ale as people could get their hands on, meaning that by the time things were under way half the street were roaring drunk and usually enjoying a mass sing-along. There wasn't a firework display, not at Canterbury bonfires – in fact, the only kind of 'display' generally on offer tended to be courtesy of whichever neighbour started fighting with another first.

Shirley had loved every single minute. Still keen to make herself useful, she went and tucked Annie's makeshift draught excluder under the back door. It was made from an old stocking stuffed with yet more newspaper – this time rolled up – and it occurred to her that Reggie's twice-a-day news-reading habit had more far-reaching benefits than she'd ever have imagined before meeting Keith. She was just pondering that revelation when her thoughts were interrupted by the sound of voices coming up the path. She went back to the front and pulled the curtain back to find it was all of them – Keith himself, David, Joe and their mam, and it tickled her as it always did how they seemed to have this collective sixth sense about when food might be getting put out, as they often seemed to drift in together.

Well, apart from Malcolm, who wasn't there because he was away from home again. He'd only been out for four months – time enough to see his brother pass away, and not a great deal more – before he was sent back to borstal for another stretch. Shirley had tried to take him under her wing for a time, believing that deep down, he surely didn't want to be involved in fighting and drinking every weekend, but apparently he did. He obviously loved it, in fact, as Keith had constantly pointed out to her. And she'd grudgingly come to accept that her attempts to get him on the straight and narrow were falling on deaf – if amused – ears. If he wasn't threatening to batter somebody, Malcolm was bored out of his brains. As her mam had speculated, he was probably too frigging clever for his own good.

No, Keith was right. He always said that Malcolm could start an argument in the mirror if there was nobody else handy, that he seemed to want to take on the world. Which made Shirley laugh, especially given that he was such a scrawny little thing, but it was a fact that the only person Malcolm was afraid of was his brother Charlie, who often had to go round the town finishing up what Malcolm had started. He would then go looking for his younger brother to give him a crack for causing mayhem, which meant Malcolm spent almost as much time trying to avoid a pasting from Charlie as giving him a reason to in the first place. But sometimes it paid off. With the amount of ale and whisky Charlie put away, if he hid for long enough it would all be forgotten.

She missed Malcolm. Yes, he was a wrong 'un, but there were flashes of goodness in there. She hoped that next time he came out he stayed out of trouble. She grinned to herself. Took a leaf out of his brother Keith's new book.

And here he was. 'I hope you've got the tea on the go, Shirl,' he said as he walked into the room, bringing the chill November air swirling in with him. He nodded behind him. 'My mam's got enough chips to feed an army here.'

'The pan's boiled and I've already put bread out,' Shirley said, wondering if she should mention that she couldn't find any butter. Young David, however, must have read her mind. 'Ta-daaa!' he said, reaching inside his school coat and pulling out a greaseproof-paper-wrapped parcel. Shirley immediately recognised the pale yellow stripe on the wrapping; it was her favourite butter. 'Here you are, Shirley,' he said. 'Put that on the table for us, will you?' He winked. He was another chip off the old block, was David. 'Left over from the last bring and buy sale,' he said. 'Been waiting best part of the week to get my hands on it.'

Shirley opened it: a lovely pat of Adams best butter. The chip sandwiches would taste much nicer now. She noticed Reggie – back behind his paper – had taken a peek above it, to see what goodies might have been purloined.

'You want some butter on your bread, Reggie?' she asked. 'Good for your bones.'

Reggie grunted. 'Aye, lass, go on. I'll have a bit. Perhaps it'll do something for my bleeding heartburn as well. Been giving me bother all bleeding day.' And as if to prove a point, he belched loudly, patting his chest with his fist as he did so.

Annie tutted. 'Do you *mind*, you mucky get!' she scolded as she tore up some extra pieces of newspaper to use as plates. 'We're just about to eat, as if you hadn't noticed.'

'Pipe down, woman' Reggie growled. 'It's better out than in.'

'You'll be out your bleeding self!' came his wife's retort, sharp as a whipcrack, causing everyone to choke on their first mouthfuls of chips. But she still made his buttie up, good and hot and buttery, and after Shirley had poured him a fresh jar of tea, she took both over to where he was sitting, thinking, as he thanked her, that she'd rarely in her life felt this content. It was Friday night at last and they'd soon have full tummies and, after a restful evening chatting and a slow walk back home, she and

Keith would be off down the Farmer Giles's coffee bar in the morning and the weekend of fun could properly begin.

No wonder she felt so at home here, she thought. Because, increasingly, this *felt* like her home.

Chapter II

January 1960

It had begun snowing in the night and it was still snowing now, so, it being a Saturday, and as Shirley wasn't meeting up with Keith till later on, she had seen no reason to leap out of bed. She was warm and cosy under her eiderdown, and despite knowing how bitter it would be once she did brave the elements to take a trip to the outdoor toilet, she was enjoying watching the florin-sized flakes drifting past her window and the soft pinkish light that snow always brought with it, which always seemed to make the world seem a kinder, gentler place.

It was gone ten by the time she'd got up and had her wash, and with the snow still falling when she'd returned to her bedroom to start getting dressed, she chose her newest black toreador trousers and a thick peach-coloured jumper. There was something relaxing about a heavy snowfall now she was too old to want to go and play in it. Now it always felt like being given permission not to rush around, and she had already half-decided she was going to spend her morning on *her*. She'd try out some new looks with her make-up, and perhaps play with hairstyles as well. After all, when she met up with Keith later on she wanted to look her best for him – plus she never knew where they might end up going. The peace wasn't destined to last, however.

'Shirley?' came the sound of her mother's voice from down-stairs. 'You dressed, love? There's someone pulling up in a car outside. Is it some of your mates? It looks like young 'uns!'

Shirley quickly smoothed down her trousers. 'Hang on, Mam – I'm coming!' she answered, pulling the jumper over her head. She didn't think it would be anyone she knew – she wasn't expecting anybody and she knew hardly anyone who had a car, but she wanted a nosey all the same. It wasn't often a car pulled up on their street – in fact it was a real rarity, because no one on Lidget Terrace owned one.

It was a little street of back-to-back houses (with two sets of outside loos serving them all) that had been originally built for the railway workers who came to Bradford several decades back, and had originally been nicknamed 'Navvy Row'. These days, however, with all the workers having long since gone back to where they'd come from, the row had been bought up by a businessman who'd sold some of them off and rented the remainder of them to tenants.

Since then it had evolved, the various residents adopting the bits of land in front of their houses and creating tiny front gardens, which they'd mostly fenced. This meant the road, such as it had ever been, was now much narrower than it should have been – no more than a track, really, made of cobblestones and dirt – no place for a car, really, snow or no snow.

She hurried downstairs to see who it might be, going straight into the front room. The gas fire was on three bars, as per usual, and the air was moist and sweltering. Her dad was sat in front of it, busy drying socks, but her mam was stationed over by the window. She had the nets up and was peering out of a circle she'd rubbed from the resulting condensation. It felt and smelt more like a Chinese laundry than a living room.

Mary turned as Shirley entered, and beckoned her over. 'It's a big green car, Shirl,' she said, 'and there's two of 'em in it. Come on. Come and look – but don't let them see you.'

Shirley laughed out loud as she walked across to where her mum was stationed. 'Mam, *honestly*!' she said, 'whoever it is out there, they're not blind, are they? You've got your nose pressed so hard against the window that you've nearly put the glass through!'

She edged her way round so she could join her mum and get a better look at the car that was carefully pulling into the tiny space outside, having presumably gone to the end and turned around first. It was a Triumph Herald; a familiar looking one, as well. One that was indeed owned by people she knew – the blonde beehive gave it away. It was, curiously, Annie and her husband Harry.

She watched them get out of the car, feeling confused. What on earth were they doing here? They had never visited before. She hadn't really even registered that Annie knew where she lived. She had no idea why they'd come, but some sixth sense told her to brace herself, and what instinct had started was finished off by getting a better look at her friend; Annie was wearing an expression that gave Shirley a horrible feeling in the pit of her stomach. Something was wrong. Something was badly wrong. She could see Annie had been crying. And, more tellingly, she didn't have a scrap of make-up on.

Shirley looked over at her dad, another instinct immediately kicking in. 'Dad, please be nice. *Please*. It's Keith's sister and her husband. And I think something's up. They wouldn't be round here otherwise. Please, Dad, okay?'

Raymond tutted as he picked up another pair of wet socks and draped them over the sleeve of his pullover. 'You'd best go let them in then, hadn't you?' he said mildly. 'I mind my own business, lass. You know that.'

Mary dropped the net curtain. 'Of course he'll be nice, pet. Tell you what, you go let them in while I pop the kettle on, eh? Ooh, I wonder what they'll think of our little house.'

Shirley shook her head in disbelief as she hurried into the hall to open the front door. There was obviously some kind of crisis going on and all her mam could think about was showing off. That was so typical of her. But more to the point, what *had* happened? A jolt of fear gripped her. Was it Keith? Had something bad happened to him? Why wasn't *he* here?

She turned the door handle, visions of accidents or visitations by police flashing across her mind's eye. He hadn't got himself into some sort of trouble, had he? The wintry air blew in a chill that entirely matched her anxious mood as she pulled the door open to let Annie and Harry in.

'Come on,' she said, taking in Annie's grey face and colourless lips. 'Come into the warm. What's going on? What's happened? I can tell something's up.'

Harry, who stood almost 12 inches above his wife, ushered her in front of him and brushed the snow from his hair, revealing the red thatch underneath. He still had one arm draped around Annie's shoulder protectively and Shirley, her eyes darting around, taking in the details, felt her heart begin thumping in her chest.

Harry finally spoke. 'It's Reggie, Shirley,' he said, shaking his head sorrowfully. 'Her dad,' he clarified. 'Reggie senior. He passed away in the early hours of this morning.'

Shirley felt her legs start to buckle beneath her. Reggie? Reggie dead? She couldn't take it in. She put her arms out and grabbed Annie, pulling her close against her, feeling the chilly wetness of the snow, which was clinging to her fur coat. 'Oh,

Annie,' she cried. 'Oh God, I'm so sorry. How did it happen? I mean, I don't understand. He was fine, wasn't he? He was fine when I saw him on Thursday. Come on,' she added, gathering her composure. 'You're like ice. Come on both of you, come through to where it's warm.'

She led the two of them into the front room and was mightily relieved when her dad stayed in his chair. In fact, his only form of greeting was a simple nod at Harry before returning his attention to his steaming socks.

Shirley didn't bother enlightening him or her mam about what Harry had just told her. They'd both have heard clearly enough, after all. Mary was already pulling out chairs from the dinner table at the back of the room, in fact. 'Here,' Shirley told Annie and Harry. 'Sit down while my mam makes you a cup of tea.'

Annie pulled a hanky from her pocket and blew her nose. 'Thanks, Shirl. I'll be all right. It's just the bleeding shock of it, that's all.'

Shirley flinched slightly, and glanced at her dad automatically. He wouldn't have stood for that kind of language on any other occasion, but thankfully he must have decided to let it go.

'Course it's a shock, Annie! Oh, how's your mam? And the rest of the family? Oh, Annie, how *awful* for you all.'

Harry pulled a packet of Woodbines and a box of matches from his pocket and Shirley cringed as she watched him light two cigarettes and pass one to Annie. She hoped he wouldn't offer her one. It was bad enough that he dared to light up in their house, let alone thinking what her dad would do if he knew *she* smoked as well. Hardly daring to meet Harry's eye in case he thought to offer the pack to her, she was just about to go to the kitchen for something to use for an ashtray when her dad beat her to it.

'Mary!' he barked, loud enough to make her jump. 'Bring a plate in for these to use. They're smoking.'

Thankfully, he didn't make the request too pointedly, and if Annie or Harry *had* noticed the slight edge in his voice neither showed it.

'Ta, love,' Annie said as Mary quickly slid a saucer in front of her. Then, as it was followed by one of Mary's best cups and saucers, she looked up and smiled a wonky smile at Shirley. 'Bleeding hell, Shirley,' she said, her eyes shiny with unshed tears, 'I feel like the bloody queen sitting here.'

The sadness in her voice was a quality new to Shirley, the brimming tears altogether unexpected, given the strength with which she'd seemed to deal with her brother Ronnie's death. It was probably true what people always said, that it was sympathy that was the killer – the thing that tipped you over when you were just about holding on. Not even 60 yet, Reggie was. It was no age to die. No surprise then that Annie was in a state of shock. But at least she was talking.

'Oh, Mam does love to impress her guests,' she said, looking pointedly at Mary, whose response was to tell her to go and fetch the custard creams. As if Annie could eat.

The tea was poured by the time she returned, everyone sipping at theirs daintily, though her dad had remained stationed with his damp socks by the fire, which, as far as Shirley was concerned, was the best place for him. He was obviously as awkward around Annie and Harry as Shirley was about them sitting round her table, and just prayed her mother didn't try to make any embarrassing small talk.

'So, what happened?' Shirley asked, placing a hand over Annie's as she sat down herself. 'And have you come here to fetch me to Keith?'

Annie nodded and sniffed. 'He said he had heartburn or indigestion or something and went off to bed yesterday afternoon. But then, through the night ...' She couldn't get any further, the tears tipping down over her pale cheeks.

'Got out of bed sometime in the night,' Harry continued. 'Collapsed on the floor clutching his chest. Their Joe came and knocked us up to go round about four – said their David had gone to phone for an ambulance.

'They were just loading him into the back when we got there. He was still alive then,' he added, reaching across to his wife to stroke her arm. 'He died on the way to St Luke's.'

'They said he had angina,' Annie added. 'I never knew. Me mam never even knew. Massive heart attack, they said. Nothing they could do.'

'Bloody hell!' Mary said, rattling her cup back onto its saucer, her choice of words not escaping Shirley's attention. Her dad would never dare pull *her* up on her language – only tut. The tea set was blue and white bone china with a pattern of forget-me-nots on it, and Shirley mused momentarily on how funny it was that the prettiest things always came out for fate's ugliest turns. 'The poor fellow,' her mam went on. 'Mrs Sykes's husband went like that as well. But, you know, love, it's not a bad way to go when you think about it. Not for him, at any rate. He wouldn't have suffered and that's a comfort at least, isn't it? How old was he, Annie, love?'

Annie started to cry harder now. 'He was only 59.' She sighed heavily. 'I think it was all just too much for him. You know ...' she added. 'What with everything that's happened down the years. Our family have had too many die. It's just not fair.'

Shirley felt tears beginning to collect in her own eyes. Poor Reggie. She'd only just really started to get to know him. She'd loved the way he'd smile at her so conspiratorially. Loved his wicked sense of humour and his banter. She tried to rein in her own thoughts – it was her job to support Annie, not wallow in her own sadness. But when the thought came to her that he'd never get to be a granddad to her and Keith's little ones, it was all she could do not to sob for him as well. Annie was right. It wasn't fair at all.

She stood up and went round to Annie's side of the table, wrapped her arms round her shoulders and hugged her hard. 'I'll go and sort my hair out while you and Harry drink your tea and we'll get off back to Canterbury, shall we? Keith'll want me there, won't he?'

Annie nodded. 'That's why we came. He's at sixes and sevens. Doesn't know quite what to do.' She smiled ruefully as she wiped her wet eyes. 'Fellas, eh? Our Margaret and Eunice might have arrived by now, too. You've not met them yet, have you?' Shirley shook her head. 'They live in Preston. So they're not too far. Our Margaret will know what to do.'

Shirley was confused. She was sure Keith had told her that their Margaret lived down in Kent. With her husband, Bob – that was it. So many names to keep track of. And … who? She racked her brains, trying to conjure the name up. Ted, that was it. Eunice's husband was called Ted. And they were older. Closer to her mam and dad's age than her own. Which was good. Without Reggie she couldn't quite imagine things. How would Keith's poor mam cope on her own?

She hurried upstairs to brush her hair, her heart full, and all thoughts of trying out new styles now vanished.

Having seen death in the family so recently, Shirley was at least partly prepared, but as Harry drove through the pretty sugar-coated streets to the comparative wasteland of Tamar Street, she felt the same welling of anxiety that she remembered feeling last time. That sense of going into something where there was nothing you could say or do that would make anything better. And when they arrived it felt worse than it had before.

Without Reggie's steadying presence, which had been so comforting when they lost Ronnie, it was almost as if supporting bricks had been removed from the walls. There was certainly an impression of everyone wandering around unsteadily – listing, as if on a ship in heavy seas, not knowing who or what to cling to.

Annie had been right. Keith was floundering – he was quiet and tight-lipped, and when she walked in he didn't even acknowledge her. Just stood staring out of the front-room window as if he hadn't even seen her. 'Are you all right, love?' Shirley asked him gently, going up to him and touching his arm. 'Do you want me to do anything?'

He looked at her blankly. 'Like what?'

He corrected himself then, presumably seeing her expression. 'Thanks, love,' he said, taking her hand and clutching it towards his chest. 'But there's nowt to do.' He nodded towards the back room where his oldest sister, Margaret, was talking to her mam and the man Shirley decided must be her husband. They had an air of authority about them. Of rolling up their sleeves and getting things done. 'Our Margaret and Bob will sort everything out,' he told her. 'The undertakers and that. The death certificate. She knows how to do all that stuff ... Thank goodness,' he added as they both became aware that whatever they were discussing with Keith's mam wasn't going too well.

In fact, they were arguing. 'Mother! I won't take no for an answer and that's that. Bugger the bloody Punch Bowl. Bugger that bloody job. You shouldn't be still working up there at your age, in any case.'

'It's only the odd shift now and again,' Annie was arguing. 'Just to keep my hand in. And I *like* working up there. It gets me out of the house.'

Keith turned around, clearly feeling that as man of the house he should have some input into what they were debating. Shirley followed him into the back room.

'What's up, Mam?' he asked mildly. 'What's the problem, our Margaret?'

His mam turned to him. 'They want me to go back to Preston with them, Keith. But I can't.' She turned back to Margaret and Bob. 'What about our Joe and David, and Keith here? Not to mention Malcolm,' she added. 'He'll be home again soon, too.'

Margaret shook her head. 'Mam, they are all big enough and ugly enough to take care of themselves. Just come for a few weeks after the funeral. That's all I'm asking. Come and rest. Let us look after you. The lads will be fine.' She turned to look at Keith then. 'You'll be all right, won't you? Course you will. You're perfectly capable. Tell Mam, Keith. *See*, Mam?' she said, not even waiting for Keith to answer. 'He's a grown man. Of *course* he'll be fine.'

Shirley bit her tongue and slipped her hand into his. Yes, Keith might be a grown man but what about Joe and David? She looked back to the front room where Keith's two youngest brothers were sitting, shell shocked, being comforted by Annie and June. They were still children, really. David especially – he was only 14. But it wasn't for her to say. Margaret had clearly got a bee in her bonnet and perhaps she was right. Perhaps Keith's mum *did* need a proper rest. But couldn't Margaret come to their house for a bit? Or Eunice, perhaps? How hard would that be? They were only in Preston, after all. But perhaps they no more wanted to live with jam jars for cups and candles for light than her own mam or dad would. And perhaps Keith's mum should have a rest from the grind of it all, too. But what about Keith? What about his needs? Her heart swelled inside her.

Still Keith said nothing. It fell to Annie senior to speak. 'Keith, would you, lad?' she asked him brokenly. 'Would you really be able to look after yourselves for a bit? Annie an' June'll be there for you, of course. And it won't be for long.'

Keith said nothing. He just nodded and it hit Shirley suddenly that his lack of an answer wasn't because he had nothing to say. It was because if he tried to speak he might cry. Which was something he couldn't do. It was his job to be a man and hold himself together, wasn't it? So she responded to the tug on her hand by letting his go, and could only look on as he resumed his station by the window.

Following his progress, and watching the way he stopped to place a gentle hand on David's head, Shirley thought that she'd never felt quite so sad. His brother gone, his dad gone, and now this – his older sister taking his mam away as well. How on earth was he going to cope? How were they all going to cope? How would they manage for money? With making sure food was on the table? With trying to keep Malcolm from going wild all over the estate once he was home?

She had no idea. She could only resolve to support the man she loved and trust in the Hudson resilience. In Reggie senior, in fact, and the strength of mind and spirit that he had hopefully passed on to his son.

* * *

Reggie's funeral was held the following Friday, and to Shirley it turned out to be a revelation. Having been to Ronnie's she expected a sombre affair, paying due respect to the departed and to those left behind – a day of reflection, grief and tears. But, as with so much when it came to the Hudsons, this funeral wasn't what she'd expected at all.

The first shock had come on the Thursday afternoon when, meeting her from work, Keith announced that they wouldn't be going home, but to have a drink for his dad up their Annie's house on Ringwood Road.

The biggest shock, however, came when she went into Annie's front room to find that Reggie's coffin was actually in there, and that when Keith said they were having a drink 'for' his dad, what he really should have said was drink 'with'. Covered in a white sheet, and with glasses and bottles dotted around the top of the coffin, Reggie was indeed in the thick of it. And even more shocking to Shirley was that nobody seemed to find this odd, that they were drinking and chatting and laughing – there was lots of laughing – with a dead body lying in their midst. Even the local Catholic priest from St Joseph's was there and drinking. She'd never been involved an anything quite so bizarre.

And it seemed the funeral itself was to follow a similar pattern. Yes, there was an outpouring of grief at the church and the cemetery, where Reggie was buried in the same grave as young Frank, his firstborn, who'd died as a toddler. But what followed, which was the wake, held at Annie and Harry's, could only be described as a knees-up. There was no less partying and drunken dancing than was seen in the Lister's on a regular Saturday night. Was this what they meant by giving a person a 'good send-off'?

It certainly seemed to be. Keith was merry in both senses of the word when they stumbled the 500 yards or so back to his.

This too would be a first – with Keith's mam going off to Margaret and Bob's straight from Annie's, she'd been given permission by her mam and dad to spend the night of the funeral at Tamar Street. And, as Keith unlocked the door and the younger boys dispersed, she knew that even if she hadn't been given permission, this would be one occasion when she would feel obliged to defy them. She didn't yet know what the future held for her and Keith now, but she knew that he would need her more than ever.

'You can have our Malcolm's bedroom,' Keith told her, for about the fourth time that evening. 'And there'll be no funny business, Shirl, I promise.' *As if*, Shirley thought. Tonight of all nights. But he was in earnest, his dark eyes glittering in the little light from the nearby street lamp. 'I just need to know you're there when I wake up tomorrow, because when this beer wears off, I think I'm going to need you.'

She kissed the top of his head, turned him around and shooed him off up the stairs, following his unsteady progress till he safely turned the corner of the landing.

She kicked off her shoes then, rolled up the sleeves of her blouse and headed into the back room to tidy up before heading to bed herself. 'Don't worry. I'll be here, my love,' she whispered.

Chapter 12

October 1961

Shirley grabbed the knocker and slammed the door as hard as she could, tears streaming in twin tracks down her face. She had no shoes on, her furious exit having taken precedence over practicality, and the cold immediately seeped into her soles. The door hadn't shut – she'd slammed it that hard that it had bounced back, as if in indignation – and she wondered fleetingly if she should take advantage of the fact and slip back inside to get them. No, she thought. No fear. She wasn't going back in there. It wasn't far to her grannie's house, in any case. So, instead, she grasped the knocker again and pushed the door further inwards. '*I hate you*, Dad!' she yelled, before slamming it again and running barefoot down the street.

It had been, without question, the best night of her life. Not least because it had begun in such an ordinary fashion, the kind of ordinary on which contented lives were built. She'd quickly freshened up her make-up and changed her shoes and Keith had met her after work. Then, despite the autumnal chill eddying around them along with the first of the fallen leaves, they'd taken a slow stroll through Horton Park to the chippy on Central Avenue, where they'd bought a fish – just the one, as they were keen to save their pennies – before walking down to meet Reggie and Vera in the Lister's Arms.

By now, Shirley felt very close to Vera and Reggie. Particularly Vera, not least because they worked together at Sutcliffe's and seemed to share the same outlook on most things in life. She also loved spending time with their two little ones, Colin and Barry, whom Keith and she would often look after and take to the park.

It had been about six o'clock by the time they'd got to the Lister's Arms. It hadn't long opened but, because it was Friday, it was already quite full. The juke-box was blaring, the weekend was beckoning, and you could almost taste the sense of fun in the air. There was only one fly in the ointment, as far as Shirley could see, and it was Keith himself. He'd gone all strange on her almost as soon as they'd arrived.

'What's wrong with you, Keith?' Shirley had eventually asked after he'd disappeared to the toilets for the third time in an hour. 'You're like a cat on hot bricks. There's not going to be any trouble, is there?'

She certainly hoped not, but she was always alert to the possibility. Thankfully, punch-ups were rarely on the agenda when it was just the four of them out, but with Keith, and particularly with his older, more confrontational brother, you never could tell when something might start. She wasn't stupid, either. She could read Keith like a book now, and seeing the brothers glancing furtively at one another put the lid on it. Something wasn't right.

'Reggie!' she snapped at him. 'Come on. What's going on? What are you two up to?' she finished, becoming more convinced by the minute. That would really make her mad, them being involved in some rumpus, when she'd been looking forward to her Friday night out all week. She looked across at Vera, because she didn't doubt she'd clocked them too, but

Vera's expression made it clear that she was as clueless about what they were up to as Shirley.

'Don't be so mental!' Keith chastised, hopping from one foot to the other in what she presumed was supposed to be a display of innocence. 'Nowt's going on, love. Just enjoy your drink and stop being so moody,' he continued. 'Frigging hell, we've come out for a good time tonight, haven't we? Not the bleeding Spanish Inquisition!'

Shirley wasn't convinced. She knew him well enough to know that his dancing feet were saying the exact opposite of his mouth, but having no choice but to accept it, she decided she would do so. Which wasn't to say she wouldn't be keeping a close eye on the pair of them, much like she'd been keeping an eye on the rest of the younger brothers just lately, in fact.

Since their mum had left for Preston after the death of Reggie senior, the house on Tamar Street had become a very different place. No longer did all the family turn up en masse with kids and significant others, and as a consequence, gone were the shouting, the laughter and the general life and soul of the place. Charlie was off in a world of his own now, his time filled with drinking, fighting and regular spells in prison. At least Malcolm had settled down a little, even had a fiancée now, Valerie, but as a consequence spent most of his time round at her mam's. Even Joe and David were living elsewhere most of the time, spending weeks on end with either friends or other family members. Which just left Keith, who these days was the only one who regularly used the house for sleeping in.

It seemed incredible that so much had changed in such a short space of time, that a family of that size and closeness could disperse in such a way. Not that they had in their hearts, she supposed, and that was what really mattered. For all the physical distance between the various members, the Hudsons were still thick as thieves, and something told her they always would be. Her now, as well.

The highlight of the evening was a local group called the Tomboys and Helen and, as Keith and Reggie knew the lead singer, Ellen, they were all keen to show their support. Shirley had seen Ellen sing before, in a band called the Dingos, so she too was looking forward to the show, and soon her anxiety about whatever it was the boys seemed so antsy about faded into the background, as the four of them caught up on their days.

The live music kicked off at nine o'clock with Chubby Checker's 'The Twist', and the effect on the pub was electrifying. People leapt up en masse and it took no more than a few seconds for the dance area to fill up and throb with movement. Where only moments before it was just the route from one part of the pub to the other, now it was a sea of jiving couples, skirts and coat-tails twirling, dotted with groups of bopping males – some confident and cool, and others self-conscious – all trying to attract the girls' attention.

Shirley felt the warmth of Keith's hand grasping her own and barely had time to put her glass down before he hauled her to her feet. 'Come on,' he said, as Reggie did likewise with Vera. 'Let's all go and have a twist, shall we?'

There were already a couple of lines forming, as was generally the case, and it was when they joined one that Shirley saw a face she thought she recognised.

'Isn't that Tommy Butler?' she asked Keith as she nodded towards one of the male singers. 'You know, the coal man who stole your Ronnie's wife?'

Shirley knew all about the day Charlie had tipped up Tommy's coal cart and the whole of Tamar Street had fallen upon the spoils. She barely needed Keith to have told her about it, either. It had passed into the realms of local folklore. Was that the issue, she wondered? That Keith and Reggie knew he'd be playing? That they were planning on giving him a pasting at some point? She hoped not. It had been years ago now, after all. But Keith's expression was benign as he nodded his confirmation. 'Yeah, it is,' he said, then presumably seeing Shirley's anxious face, added, 'Don't worry, Shirl. We're letting bygones be bygones – he's not a bad bloke these days, as it happens.'

Shirley felt relief wash over her. Perhaps she'd been imagining things earlier, then; seeing things that weren't there. Perhaps it was going to be good night after all. Her Keith was certainly mellowing. There was no doubt about it. If he'd been after a fight tonight, then surely he would have started trouble with Tommy. And their Reggie wouldn't have been far behind him. The Hudsons were big on retribution, no matter how many years had passed. It was one of the things that made the family so notorious.

But not tonight. And after a few numbers, the four of them took a break, and as they headed to the bar, glistening with sweat, breathing heavily, Shirley felt the cares of the working week melt away. There was nothing quite like dancing to make you happy, she decided as they shouldered their way to a space at the bar and Reggie ordered them all fresh halves of bitter. And with the place fairly buzzing now, there was almost as much fun to be had just by standing at their vantage point, with its great view of the stage, and watching others spinning round and having fun.

Keith sipped the top off his half and winked at her. Despite the exertion of the dancing, he didn't seem to have a hair out of place. 'Best stay here for a bit now,' he advised, 'hang on to our spot. If we don't it'll take ages to get served again.'

Shirley nodded. She was happy to stand, having been sitting at her machine all day, and was content just to watch and listen for a while. It was a chance to talk girl-talk with Vera as well – if Annie was the twin sister she'd always wished she had, Vera really was the older one, full of wisdom, her Colin and Barry the surrogates for the kids she couldn't wait to have herself.

'How's your new house coming along, V?' Shirley asked her. 'Keith said your Reggie is building a bar in the front room. Very posh, I must say. Whoever heard of it? A proper *bar* in a person's house!'

Vera smiled. 'Oh, it's not even his first, Shirl. We had one in our last house as well. He's good with his hands is my Reg.' She nudged Shirley. 'And in more ways than one, and all,' she finished, grinning.

Shirley felt herself colouring. She couldn't stop herself. She was getting used to the way the Hudsons were so open about certain matters, but it still embarrassed her when the girls said things like this. She hoped Vera wouldn't notice in the dim light spilling from the bar wall, because she didn't want to seem the innocent that she was. She hoped not. And she wondered if she'd feel less self-conscious when she eventually gave up her virginity for the man she loved. She doubted it; her mam had done a good job of drilling it into her that some things were private and not to be spoken about. 'You don't let any man put his pencil in your notebook, Shirley,' she'd told her. 'Not till you're sure that if he puts a bun in your oven he's going to do the decent thing and marry you.'

Shirley had never been sure how you could *ever* be sure – not about something like that. She trusted Keith completely, but she wasn't silly. Men were men, weren't they? And she heard too much down at Sutcliffe's not to know that some of them could sweet-talk you into going all the way with them then turn around and let you down at the drop of a hat.

Not that she'd ever feel able to chat to her mum about things like that anyway. That had been the one and only time sex had ever been hinted at in their house, and Shirley still cringed at the thought of her mam and dad knowing such things. And as for *doing* such things together – yuck!

The music stopped at ten o'clock, prompting the girls to stop chatting, and the singer, Ellen, took the mic in her hand. 'I hope you're all having a great night, boys and girls!' she said. 'And now I'd like to bring up a guest singer. I've sang with his sister Annie many times,' she went on, causing Shirley to turn around, realising what was happening, 'but tonight, boys and girls, I give you … KEITH HUDSON!'

Keith leant to kiss her cheek as he placed his beer back down on the bar, and as the crowd clapped and parted so he could make his way to the stage, she felt herself blushing all over again. It never changed. However many times she watched him sing at the Lister's she still found it as excruciating as she found it enjoyable, both because she knew girls were scrutinising her as well, and because, well, because she loved him and it made her tummy squirm to think he might forget his words.

Which was ridiculous, she knew, because he never forgot his words. She sometimes thought he must have been born on a stage, already singing. As their Annie had once told her when they were watching him a few months back, he had natural charisma. Shirley smiled to herself as she watched Keith saunter to the stage and grab the microphone, remembering Annie's follow-up observation about her brother – 'and you'd better keep an eye on the girls down the front, because we both know what the little bleeders would like to do with him'.

'Thanks, Ellen,' Keith said now, turning his gaze towards the bar. 'I'm singing this for Shirley. Let's hope I remember the words,' he said, almost as if he'd read her mind. He grinned at everyone. 'Now, I've had a few.'

The crowd laughed and applauded as the music started up, and, for only the second time in the three years they'd been together, Shirley recognised the familiar strains of her favourite Anthony Newley song. She felt the hairs stand up on her neck. Keith was going to sing 'Why'.

It was difficult to watch, because the tears sprang so quickly to Shirley's eyes, and instead of giggling and calling her a wet for being so sentimental, Vera's eyes, she noticed, filled up as well. And as Keith reached the close of the song and started to walk across to her, still singing, she was torn between wanting the ground beneath her to swallow her up and running towards him and flinging her arms around him. As it was, hugely embarrassed now, she just stayed rooted to the spot as the song finished and the crowd roared their approval. And then, seeing Keith's silence, they seemed to act as a single being, shutting their mouths, stilling their hands, watching and waiting, while Shirley, transfixed, held her breath.

Keith suddenly dropped down onto one knee before her. 'Shirley,' he said quietly, 'will you marry me?'

The tears kept coming now as well. She could feel the wetness of them slipping down her neck as she gulped in lungfuls of cold autumn air. The best night of her life. The best night she'd *ever* had. And now her bloody dad was threatening to ruin it all.

He'd not let it be, either, even now she'd left. He'd pushed open the front window, determined to have the last word. 'And if he's hiding up the road,' he'd roared, 'you can tell him that an' all, Shirley! Not a cat in hell's chance, you hear me?'

The window had slammed shut then, blocking out her retort. Why was her dad so bloody stupid? So bloody stubborn? She sobbed her frustration. Well, she could be stubborn too! And she bloody would be. She'd spent her whole life having to submit to his rules and regulations, but standing there now, on Lidget Terrace, her feet growing numb, she thought back to the little girl who'd had the strength to defy him – to him appearing in her life, to those long hours at the table, to the will she had then and still had now.

She stopped running and looked up and down Lidget Terrace, reflecting on the choices she now had. The little street of back-to-backs now housed quite a lot of her family. Her mam and dad had number 5, Granny Wiggins was at number 9, her Auntie June – Mary's sister – now lived at number 6, and just two months ago, to her delight, Reggie and Vera had moved in too – cocking a snook at her dad and his holier-than-thou ways by buying and doing up number 11. Rubbing her eyes, she made a decision. It wasn't fair to bring her grannie or Auntie June into this. No, she'd go where it was right to go – into the arms of her fiancé, who was indeed hiding up at number 11.

'Oh, love, what *is* it?' Vera asked, concerned, as Shirley pushed the door open, the tears of frustration and anger springing once again as she saw Keith's anxious face.

'I take it your dad wasn't too happy, then?' Keith asked, pulling her against him, while Vera went to make a pot of tea.

Shirley cried hard into his shoulder for some time. 'What can we *do*?' she sobbed eventually. 'I can't marry you, Keith – not without both them agreeing. Dad's got to sign the papers, hasn't he?'

'Look at your feet!' Vera gasped as she came back into the room. 'What were you thinking! You'll catch your death. Here,' she said, kicking off her slippers. 'Have these. And don't you worry, love,' she added. 'I'm sure he'll come round eventually. Once he knows you mean it, he will. My dad did in the end.'

Shirley wasn't so sure. Vera didn't know what her dad was like, did she? He was as stubborn as they came. She pushed her feet into Vera's slippers and accepted the tea gratefully, but the gloom that had descended wouldn't shift. It was all wrong. She was an adult, near as good as. How could he do that? And didn't he *want* to see her happy?

She was just about to say so when there was a noise outside the house, closely followed by the appearance of her mam in the front room, hands on hips and looking like she was about to crack someone.

'Mam!' Shirley cried, leaping up and nearly spilling her tea. Oh, God, she thought. She hoped she wasn't going to show her up. 'What are you doing here? Where's my dad? Is he with you?'

Her mother tutted. 'Never mind him,' she retorted irritably. 'He's sat at home drying bleeding socks, as per usual!' She glanced at Vera. 'I'll have a cup of that tea, love, if you've some in the pot still. I'm knackered with all the running about.'

Shirley was confused. She'd only left her house half an hour ago, if that. What could possibly have happened in that space of time?

A lot, it seemed. 'I've just come back from your granny's,' Mary explained as she sat down, breathing hard, on Vera's posh new couch. 'Anyway, the long and the short of it is that *I'm* going to sign for you.'

'What – to get *married*?' Keith asked her, sounding shocked.

As he would. She couldn't do that. It wasn't legal. 'But, Mam, you can't. We need Dad to sign as well,' Shirley told her.

'Let me bloody finish, will you, girl!' Mary snapped. 'You fetch me the papers and I'll do the signing. Mine *and* his. I can do his signature, bleeding misery guts that he is. And if he finds out, it's tough titties, isn't it?'

Keith gaped. 'You'd really do that?' he asked Shirley's mam, his face lighting up. He looked at Shirley, and she could tell he was looking at her mam with a new respect. He grinned then, and flung his arms round her, nearly spilling his tea as well. 'So you *will* go to the ball after all, love!'

Shirley knew how he felt. That her mam would do that for them – it made tears well in her eyes all over again. 'Oh, Mam, thanks so much,' she said, putting her tea down and giving Mary a hug. 'But won't it cause hell between you and my dad? I mean, he *will* find out, won't he? How can he not know? *Course* he will.'

Mary's frown became a smile. 'You leave the old bugger to me,' she said. 'And that's not all. I've got even better news for you both.'

She paused to sip her tea then, her eyes suddenly alive with mischief. 'Come on, Mam, tell us!' Shirley urged.

'Well, like I said, I've been running about, haven't I?' They all nodded. 'And the last place I went was your granny's, just now. And me and her have sorted everything out for you.'

She looked at Shirley and Keith in turn. '*What*, Mam?' Shirley wanted to know. 'What have you sorted out?'

'That the pair of you can have number 17.'

Shirley looked at Keith in confusion and then back to Mary. 'Number 17? What, *here*? In Lidget Terrace? What do you mean?'

'It's for sale at £165,' Mary explained. 'And as me and your granny have paid Mr Taylor religiously for years, he's said we can buy number 17 for you and Keith. No deposit, so you won't need to worry about that or anything. A pound a week.' She looked at Keith. 'You can manage that, can't you, love? I know it'll be tight, but it's a good start. You'll be buying your first house.'

Shirley couldn't take it in. They could actually buy a *house*? Just like that? It seemed almost too incredible to be true. But it clearly was true; her mam was sat there, real as day, even asking Vera if she had any biscuits to go with the tea. So it had to be true. It *was* true. No pinching required.

She'd been wrong. Last night might have been the best night of her life, but today, she decided, had topped it. Her mam was back talking to her. Talking to both her and Keith, in fact. She took her fiancé's hand and hugged it tight.

'Oh, Mam, she said, 'Thank you *so* much. You know I love you, don't you?'

Mary grinned. 'Course I do, pet, and I love you too. But you need to crack on and get hold of those papers for me to sign, before your dad gets wind of what's happening with the house. Oh, and another thing. Mr Taylor said you can have the keys to it next week, so you can both get on and start prettying the place up a bit. But one thing ...' she looked mostly at Keith as she spoke. 'There'll be no living under the brush, mind. You don't move in there till your married, okay?'

Shirley squeezed Keith's hand again and felt the answering pressure. It was all she could do not to giggle like a schoolgirl at what she knew was going through both their minds. 'Till I'm Mrs Hudson,' she said, the words feeling delicious on her tongue. And the sooner the better. She was counting the days.

Chapter 13

January 1962

Shirley stood outside the Blue Lion on Manchester Road and stopped to catch her breath. She couldn't remember the last time she'd been so fuming. Not least because she'd just put her valuable Saturday job in jeopardy, and whose fault was that? Frigging *Keith's.*

What made her even crosser was that she felt she'd been duped, and it was a feeling that had begun to really gnaw at her as she'd stomped the half hour's journey from the fruit stall on John Street Market to the pub she'd now entered on Manchester Road. Two months till their wedding! How frigging dare he? Two months, and her working her frigging fingers to the bone; she'd be rattling around like a skeleton in her dress at this rate!

'It'll be such a help,' Keith had said to her, just after Christmas, when the possibility of helping on the fruit stall every Saturday had come up. A friend of their Annie's had told him about it and he thought it was a brilliant idea. 'It'll help pay for the buffet, won't it, Shirl?' he'd added. And she'd had to concede that was true. 'Not only that,' he'd gone on, but you'll be able to nick a bit of fresh fruit and veg for me, won't you? Do me good. I tell you, Shirl, I'm struggling a bit in that house all by myself.'

Shirley hated both ideas. She didn't want to take the job and she certainly didn't want to take the fruit – and probably wouldn't – but she did concede that it probably made sense. Money was tight and though she already worked long shifts at Sutcliffe's, it wouldn't hurt to do a few extra hours on a Saturday to help with the costs of their upcoming nuptials. And it felt only fair. Poor Keith had been working like mad since her mam had got them the keys for number 17 – couldn't have worked harder if he'd tried. Him and their Reggie had done a lovely job as well. They'd decorated their little one-up, one-down so beautifully that she almost had to catch her breath every time she went in there, realising that this beautiful home was going to be all their own.

It was almost done now, as well, most of the furniture in, too; she couldn't wait to show off their beautiful green couch and the new double bed she was particularly proud of, with its huge spring mattress and the beautiful, shiny wooden head and foot boards. She hadn't asked where either of these items had appeared from, but suspected that it had something to do with Malcolm, who was now back out of prison – and for good this time, it seemed, because he was now settling down (and hopefully calming down) with Valerie. They'd plenty of blankets, sheets and curtains, too, courtesy of Mary, and she was counting the days till she and Keith could move into their own little palace, especially now her dad was beginning to come round to it all.

Not that it had been an easy process. Although Raymond had stuck to his guns, even after Mary had forged his signature, he had eventually taken on board that she and Keith were getting married whether he liked it or not. After all, as Shirley had pointed out till she was sick of hearing herself saying it, by the time they married, Shirley would be 21 anyway, so wouldn't even need their consent.

Still, as far as Raymond was concerned, no man would ever be good enough for his little girl, and no matter how persuasive Mary had been, he still wasn't entirely happy. Perhaps he never would be. Though Christmas had reaped unexpected rewards on that front, during a family get-together at Granny Wiggins's. Keith and Shirley had been there, were there along with Mary's sisters, Edna and June, and, of course, Mary and Raymond had been there, too. Everyone had been drinking when, out of the blue, since no one thought she was anywhere near enough gone, Shep, Granny's dog, had gone into labour, and started giving birth to a litter of puppies.

'Come along, you youngsters,' Granny Wiggins had said, cool as a cucumber, and a slightly pickled one at that. 'Soon as they're out, you're to take them to the water butt and drown them.'

Shirley didn't think she'd ever been quite so horrified. Yes, she knew it was standard practice – they were mouths that her granny couldn't afford to feed, and with no one around to take them off her hands, it was the 'kindest' thing. Lots of others of her generation did just the same, and it wasn't as if it was the first time. Granny Wiggins always drowned Shep's puppies. But Shirley couldn't help it; she wanted no part in it – seeing them born and, even as Shep was giving birth to more of them, taking them and killing them? It upset her so much she'd had to run from the room in floods of tears.

Keith had come into his own then. 'Hang on, *we* want one of those puppies,' he told Granny Wiggins, despite Shirley knowing full well they could ill-afford to have one, even if Keith had wanted one, which he didn't. It had been something they'd already discussed.

'No, you don't,' Shirley's gran had said, though she knew no such thing. 'You can no more look after a pup than I can, lad. Eat you out of house and home in no time.'

'We'll manage,' he'd said, with an edge in his voice that Shirley knew meant business. 'Let her keep one and wean it, and we'll take it off you soon as it's ready.' And though she was thrilled her gran had conceded she'd known from the way Keith had looked at her that if she'd said no, he'd have probably taken it anyway and weaned it himself.

And, unlikely as it might have seemed, it had touched a chord with her dad, who always hated that her gran drowned Shep's puppies. He'd not said much, but then he hadn't needed to. Just placed a hand on Keith's shoulder as he'd gone home that night. 'You're a good lad,' he'd said quietly.

Everything had changed since that day. And for the better. But there were other changes that needed making, clearly.

Although she'd at first baulked at having to get up so early on a Saturday morning, the fruit market had by now become like a second home to Shirley, and she'd come to look forward to her weekly stint there. There was such a colourful mix of characters, both manning the stalls and buying from them, and she'd made lots of friends that she'd started seeing socially, as well. She generally hung out with three girls from nearby stalls, Moira, Magdalen and Sheila, who she'd invariably meet up with at Pie Tom's during their late-morning break, for a cold drink, a portion of mushy peas and a natter. They would gossip about anything and everything: their boyfriends, their clothes and hairdos, what they'd be doing that night, and generally they would have a good laugh.

Today, however, Shirley wasn't happy. Not when Moira filled her in on what she'd just seen, at any rate.

'What do you mean they were covered in blood?' she asked. Moira had just joined them, as she wasn't starting till 12 today, and had just walked down to John Street with her other half.

And apparently seen something that made Shirley's blood boil.

'I'm telling you, Shirley,' Moira said as she lit a cigarette, 'me and my Chiggy were walking down Manchester Road, and there they both were, staggering up it. Your Keith and Malcolm – it was definitely them – laughing and carrying on, covered in blood.' She paused to exhale smoke. 'I'm sure Malcolm had a tooth missing – looked like it, anyway. But don't worry – your Keith looked all right.'

Whatever feelings of concern came into Shirley's head were fleeting. And spirited away altogether by Moira's next utterance, that she'd seen them both heading into the Blue Lion.

Anger bubbled up inside her. This was becoming something of a habit, despite the deal they'd struck when she'd agreed to take the Saturday job; that while she was working hard – to pay for the frigging buffet, like he'd wanted – he would under no circumstances be spending the money before she'd even earned it, out drinking and gambling with his brothers – something that, just lately, he'd been reneging on.

'I'll bleeding kill him!' she huffed. And she meant it as well. He'd promised her faithfully that he wouldn't be in the pubs today, only the previous evening. Said he was going to spend the day cleaning the windows for the residents of Lidget Terrace – to earn a few bob to take them out *tonight*. Said he'd be at it all day till it was time to get washed and come and meet her at the market when she knocked off at half four. 'The little pillock!' she added, shaking a cigarette out of her packet and grabbing Moira's matches. 'He promised he wouldn't drink till he met me later! Right, that's it,' she said, changing her mind and putting the ciggie back in the packet. 'Two can play at that bloody game.'

There was a ripple of oohs and ahs among the girls as she stood up and started to untie her apron strings. 'Hey, what you going to do, Shirl?' Magdalen asked her.

Shirley grinned, feeling a keen sense of anticipation rush through her. And something like excitement as well. 'Well, Magdalen,' she said, rolling up her pinny and giving it to Moira, you can tell the boss that I've got an emergency and had to go. If he doesn't like it, he can shove it up his arse for all I care. I'm off to go and teach Keith a little lesson.'

The girls looked impressed, if slightly nervous about this unexpected turn of events. 'That's not like you, Shirley,' Moira pointed out. 'What on earth you going to do?'

'I don't actually know yet,' Shirley admitted. 'But if it's beer and a fight he prefers to doing right by me, then he can have one. I haven't spent all this time around his family without learning how to give him that!'

She took a deep breath before pushing the doors open and going into the Blue Lion. It wasn't a pub they used every week but at least she knew it well enough to know the landlord and most of the customers, who were also regulars at the Lister's and the Bull at Little Horton.

She saw them as soon as she entered. Saw and heard them, more to the point, because they were clearly holding court; sitting in the corner, both holding pints, and surrounded by quite a gathering – friends, male and female, who were clustered around, their backs to Shirley, obviously engrossed on whatever her silly fiancé and his feckless brother had to say.

It served her purpose well. Even if either of them had been able to get a glimpse of her as she slipped inside, they were clearly much too wrapped up in themselves to take any notice.

Which left her free to calmly walk past the Saturday drinkers to the bar and turn her back on them – though with the Hudson brothers holding court, probably with some tale of great bravery, she knew she was as good as invisible anyway. She would soon put a stop to that, as well.

She smiled at Billy, the landlord. 'Two pints of bitter, please.'

'Hello, Shirley, love,' he said, returning her smile. Then he nodded towards the little retinue in the corner. 'I'd just get your own, love,' he advised. 'Keith and Malcolm have already got pints.' He leaned forwards slightly. 'And they've already had a fair few, lass.'

Shirley smiled again. She was quite enjoying this – perhaps it was the adrenalin coursing through her. 'That's all right, Billy,' she said. 'Just the two pints, please, as I said. I'm going to surprise them with another.'

Billy laughed as he pulled them. 'No wonder he's marrying you, lass. What a bird, you are!'

There was no answer to that. And she was all done with smiling. Or laughing, for that matter. Because this was *no* laughing matter. She felt a fresh wave of anger rise inside her; right at this moment, she wasn't in the mood to talk weddings. 'Thanks, Billy,' she said politely as she curled her hands round both the glasses and turned around.

She was about to head towards them, but she checked herself. She could see more of Keith now – though there was obviously no danger of him seeing her. Obviously the centre of attention, he only had eyes for his audience. He was indeed caked in blood – dried blood – and his shirt was ripped open, and Malcolm, next to him, was obviously revelling in the telling of their earlier adventures. 'You should have seen him,' Malcolm roared, loud enough to carry right across to her, 'that bleeding Spare Rib went down like a sack of spuds! One punch and' – he mimed it – 'down he went!'

Shirley knew Spare Rib. He was another of the characters that frequented most of the local pubs and bars. Her mouth set in a tight line, she listened as he continued. It wouldn't have taken much, she thought. Poor bloody Spare Rib. He was tiny – even smaller than the Hudson lads.

'And then, out of nowhere,' Malcolm continued, 'comes these two big bruisers. Built like brick shithouses, the pair of them. Spare Rib, still rolling on the floor, and me and our Keith looked at each other – didn't we, Keith?'

Keith nodded and took up the story. 'Well, you know me,' he said, to an obviously gratifying chorus of agreement, 'I just thought, in for a penny, in for a pound! I nodded at our Malcolm, and we just dived in, didn't we? I thought we were gonners at first – who bleeding wouldn't?' More miming, presumably, Shirley thought, of what a brick shithouse looked like. 'But it turned out they were all brawn and no brains. They never saw one punch coming, not one. Anyway,' he finished, sitting back on the seat, his shirt gaping suggestively, 'we left 'em in the Lister's splattered on the deck, and came up here.'

Shirley had seen and heard enough. Had had enough even before she clocked the two women simpering around Keith and Malcolm, obviously far from oblivious to their heroic charms, despite – or perhaps because of – their dishevelled state. Particularly that of her good-looking soon-to-be husband – batting their eyelashes and, if Shirley wasn't mistaken, giggling like a pair of schoolgirls, rather than the ageing muck 'ooks they undoubtedly were. She wasn't having that.

'Listen, love,' she said as she approached the busty blonde who was apparently about to sit down next to Keith, 'I wouldn't park yourself next to my boyfriend if I were you, unless you want to end up as bloody as he is. You understand?'

The blonde began forming her features into a pugnacious expression but, presumably seeing Shirley's, changed her mind. She and her friend quickly tottered off, leaving Malcolm and Keith staring open-mouthed at Shirley, apparently arrived out of nowhere and clutching two beers.

'Shirley, love,' Keith slurred, 'I was just coming to meet you. Did you finish early?'

The small gathering also started to disperse now, and seeing the two of them close up made Shirley even angrier.

'I've jacked the job in, for your information,' Shirley barked at him, 'You bleeding arsehole! You just couldn't stay out of trouble, could you? The minute you're out with *him*' – she nodded towards Malcolm – 'all your bleeding promises go straight out of the window.'

'Hey!' Malcolm said, beginning to laugh, albeit a bit nervously. 'Don't be blaming me, Shirl. *He's* the oldest here. Old enough to do what he wants, an' all. Face it,' he drawled, warming to his theme now, 'you'll never have that one under your thumb, love. He's an 'udson.'

Shirley was shaking. Actually shaking all over, she was now that angry. 'Oh, is that *right*, Malcolm?' she asked, pleased to see him blink in surprise at her rejoinder. 'Well, let me spell something out for you, shall I? As of March, *I'll* be a bleeding Hudson as well, so I might as well start acting like the bleeding rest of you!'

She threw the two pints with all the force she could muster. One straight at Keith, the other towards Malcolm, and in such a temper that she didn't give a hoot for the consequences. Which were, despite her rage, just what she'd hoped for. Each glass hit each Hudson brother square on the head, smashing

with a satisfying explosion of glass and sound, and showering
both surprised brothers in beer.

The pub became silent as the yeasty smell pervaded the air.
But perhaps it had been quiet from the moment she'd spoken,
Shirley reflected, as she stood there, feeling the stares drilling
into her back. She didn't care. Rather than blush, as she
normally would, she felt a rush of satisfaction. Not to mention
pride, almost, which pleased her even more. She leaned forward
and tipped over the table for good measure, causing the
contents of their own glasses to spill onto them too. Then she
turned and strode through the pub back to the entrance, and
turned back only once before walking out into the cold afternoon air. 'And by the way,' she shouted, to everyone and no
one in particular, 'I wouldn't take any notice of what those two
have been telling you. They probably got battered, the pair of
them – they both think they're ten men when they've had a
few.'

Shirley glared towards her fiancé and his feckless little
brother. 'Only trouble is, they bleeding aren't!'

Shirley walked back to Clayton feeling strangely euphoric, her
stride purposeful and rhythmic and her head held high.
Something had changed in her, something fundamental, and
she liked it a lot. No more would she be a doormat – not for
anyone, ever – and no more would she keep her trap shut if she
had something to say.

It had been a stressful few months for her, no doubt about it.
What with organising the wedding, dealing with her dad and
everything else, Shirley knew she was almost at breaking point.
Keith had left everything to her and her mam to do – the
church, the bridesmaids, the dress, the catering, the invites,
everything. All he'd done was assure her that he didn't care

what she did. 'Just as long as I get to marry the love of my life, Shirl,' he'd said.

At first she'd been touched by his romantic pronouncement. 'Oh, Mam,' she'd said to Mary, 'isn't that just the loveliest thing to say?'

But it had taken more than her mother's sceptical expression to make her realise that, actually, Keith had played a bit of a blinder. He'd set it up perfectly – to enable him to get away with doing frig all! Not that that mattered now; things were almost all organised anyway. But it did add grist to the mill and serve to strengthen her resolve about how things were going to be from here on. He was going to grow up a bit, that was what was going to happen. She'd make sure of it, if it was the last thing she did.

Though right now, she thought as she turned into Lidget Terrace, he'd best keep right out of her way. She glanced at her own snow-white nets as she headed up to her mam's house, hoping Keith would have more sense than to return there tonight. She hoped he might end up at Malcolm's house back in Buttershaw rather than taint their new home with his blood-ied clothes, his hangover and his stupid, pissed-up brother, and wouldn't dare darken her mam's doorway till the morning. Oh, she knew he'd be all apologetic the next day – he always was. She just hoped – and resolved – that by this time tomorrow, she'd be strong enough not to succumb to his charms, immedi-ately fall into his arms and forgive him. That was important. He needed to learn that she wasn't ever going to be a pushover; that she'd never put up with what she'd seen for herself where his brothers' wives were concerned.

She was learning. She'd been learning since she'd first joined the family. That if you were a Hudson lad you were the boss, almost by definition. And that if you were a Hudson *girl*, you were always the boss as well. But if you married into the family – boy or girl, it didn't matter – you were expected to be the underdog.

Well, not this girl.

Chapter 14

Shirley was pacing the floor in her mam's living room. It had been two weeks since her run-in with Keith in the pub and it was something she wouldn't forget in a hurry. Already tagged the 'showdown at the Blue Lion corral', it was something she recalled with both pride and a giggle, not least because only last night – the first time she'd felt brave enough to go in the pub since – she realised she'd become as notorious as certain members of her fiancé's family. Having reassured her that he was on her side and that she'd done exactly the right thing, Billy the landlord had then served her and Keith's drinks, and put her half of bitter in a plastic glass. 'Just to be on the safe side,' he'd joked.

Not that Shirley was still at odds with Keith – far from it. He'd learned his lesson, as she'd known he would (as would that little tyke Malcolm, for that matter) and as, luckily, there'd been no damage done, except to his pride, all was once again peace and harmony between them.

Keith had worked hard to make amends, too. He'd been beavering away at their new house for most evenings since and earlier in the week had presented her with an enormous bunch of daffodils. That was the clincher in terms of an apology, as far as Shirley was concerned – even if he continued to swear blind he'd been too drunk to remember the ins and outs of any of it.

She was also having a rare day off from her Saturday job, so she'd felt particularly good when she'd jumped out of bed this morning. Better than good, in fact, and not just because of the excitement of the coming wedding; no, today was going to be something of a red-letter day in itself: Keith had, it seemed, acquired a car.

Shirley couldn't have been more excited if she'd tried. And it was obviously showing. 'You're going to wear that bloody carpet out in a minute, lass!' her dad admonished, as she kept going to the window to check the street for any sign of Keith's appearance. 'Why don't you go make me a pot of tea instead? He'll be here when he gets here. Gawping down the street won't bring him any quicker. And I don't doubt we'll hear him coming before we see him, in any case. And, if we don't, pound to a penny your mother will.'

Her dad was probably right, Shirley conceded, because Keith would be arriving in style; all being well, he'd be picking her up in it. He'd got it from his boss, Peter Canning, whose house he'd been decorating in his spare time these past few weeks, and which Mr Canning had given to him in lieu of extra wages.

Shirley couldn't quite believe it – she and Keith were actually going to have a car! There weren't many people who could say that round their part of Bradford. She knew they'd be the envy of all their friends, most of whom hadn't even passed their driving tests. Keith had been lucky in that regard, having passed his years back, while in the army, but she'd never dreamed he'd actually be able to put it to use – not yet.

But that had just been the first bit of exciting news he'd had to share with her the previous evening. He wasn't just coming round to pick her up and take her for a bit of a spin. They were actually heading off on a bit of a holiday for a few days, going to their Margaret and Bob's over in Preston.

'To Preston? In January?' Raymond had muttered when she'd told him the previous evening, keen to obtain his permission so that she could actually go. 'Who the bleeding hell wants to go on holiday to Preston in January?' he wanted to know. 'At any time, in fact. You must want your head testing.'

'*They* do,' Mary had pointed out. 'To stay with Keith's sister. And a very nice time I don't doubt they'll have as well. They can go to Blackpool.' She'd sighed wistfully. 'Oh, I'd *love* to go back to Blackpool.'

'In *January*, woman?' Raymond had persisted. 'Then you need your head testing as well.'

But at least he'd agreed to it – well, based on Shirley's promise that they wouldn't be sharing a bedroom, anyway – and now she was packed and they were actually going, she felt a swell of excitement at the thought of them driving off together like a proper married couple.

Not that it was going to be a holiday in the usual sense. They were going to Preston, first and foremost, to collect Keith's mam and bring her home, to give his elder sisters a much-needed break from having to look after her all this time. Not that Shirley cared what the reason was. She was just pleased to be going anywhere. Growing up, she'd been used to doing an annual trip to Blackpool with her mam and dad, but since she'd started work at 16, she hadn't been away anywhere. Apart from the odd concert she'd attended with her mate, Anita, she'd barely put a foot outside of Bradford, in fact.

They were definitely returning to Blackpool as well, whatever else they did with their time. It wasn't very far – only about 17 miles from Preston – and Keith had promised her a day out there, and she couldn't wait to go on some rides, eat fish and chips and have some fun. She'd packed her winter woollies, too, because what she was looking forward to the most was being able to have a romantic stroll along the fairy-lit pier with him, arm in arm. She could almost smell the candy floss and the sharp, salt-laden breeze. She certainly didn't care what the weather did.

'Here you go, Dad,' she said as she passed Raymond his chipped pint pot of tea. 'You didn't hear a car pull up, did you?'

Raymond lowered the paper he'd been reading. 'Shirley, when he gets here, you'll know about it.' He cast his eyes towards the ceiling. 'You know what your mam's like – she might be reckoning to be changing the bed up there, but as sure as eggs is eggs she'll have her nose glued to that bedroom window. You mark my words, you'll hear her when he gets here.'

They did so too, almost as soon as he'd got the words out, from the sound of her mam clattering down the concrete steps to the kitchen.

'Shirley!' she called, 'Keith's here! Oh, you should see the car, love! Oh, it's a little beauty, it really is!'

She popped her head round the living-room door, almost as excited as Shirley was, before disappearing again, presumably to open the front door.

Shirley followed, as did her dad, after carefully putting his tea down, and soon all three were spilling out onto the street to see his new toy in the flesh. Shirley wasn't sure what constituted a 'little beauty' in car terms and, given that Keith had acquired it for no more than a few days' hard graft, she wondered quite how beautiful it could possibly be. Still, she thought, as Keith revved it, sending clouds of grey smoke down the street, she'd find out soon enough, wouldn't she?

He turned off the engine and the car shuddered into silence. 'Are you sure it's going to be all right, Keith?' Shirley asked, fanning her face as he clambered out to join them. 'Only there seems to be an awful lot of smoke coming out of it.'

Keith was grinning from ear to ear as he shut the driver's door – the proverbial Cheshire cat. He then went round the front and patted the bonnet affectionately. 'Course she is, Shirl. She's a 1949 Ford Popular. Safe as houses, she is. My boss told me she'll run for ever.'

It was dark green and curvy, with a front that Shirley decided looked almost like a face. Wistful-looking, eyes on stalks, a little like an eager-to-please sheepdog. And old and worn, she thought, eyeing it suspiciously; as was also the case with her mum's comment about it being a little beauty, she was equally uncertain that she and Keith shared the same idea about what the words 'for ever' might mean.

But it had got him here, hadn't it? And his excitement was certainly infectious. And, as her dad had said already, a car *was* a car – it represented freedom of a kind she'd never had. They could go anywhere. *Anywhere*. Well, provided they could afford the petrol. Which was as thrilling a thought as she'd had in a long time. No more trams, no more buses, no more trains. She turned to Raymond now. 'What d'you think? Do you like it, Dad?' she asked him hopefully.

Raymond drew a hand over the nearest wheel arch as if checking a sideboard for dust. There was never any danger of him seeming too enthusiastic, even if he was. And given he'd never owned a car himself – or ever wanted to, for that matter – Shirley wasn't expecting him to wax that lyrical about it. She just hoped he'd pronounce it good enough to transport her to Preston and to help lift Keith a little further in his ever-critical eyes. 'I don't know much about cars, lass,' he said finally. 'But it got him here from Listerhills, didn't it?' He winked at Keith. 'So I suppose it'll be all right.'

'Oh, it's *lovely*, Keith,' Mary enthused, looking hopefully up and down the street. 'Did the neighbours look out as you drove

past, Keith, love? I bet they did. That Beryl up the road's
daughter's boyfriend can't even *drive* yet. Get in it, girl,' she
added, pushing Shirley in the direction of the passenger door
Keith had now opened. 'Go on, hurry up. If they're looking out
I want them all to know whose it is.'

'Oh, Mam!' Shirley said, refusing to play the usual game.
'Who even bloody cares? Besides, they'll know soon enough
because you'll tell them, won't you? Chances are you'll have
told half of Clayton before we've even left the city.' She turned
to Keith, then, who was lovingly brushing specks of dirt from
the windscreen. 'Are we ready to go, love? I've packed my suitcase. I'll have Dad fetch it out, shall I?'

'Hark at you,' Keith laughed, affecting a plum-in-the-
mouth voice. 'Gone all posh now you can travel in style, have
you? You sound just like that daughter from *Dixon of Dock
Green*. Shall Daddy pack the car for one, too, while he's about
it?'

An hour later, the flush of excitement Shirley had carried with
her all morning was a little more tempered by reality. It was
lovely being snuggled up close to Keith as he drove, certainly,
marvelling at the driving prowess she'd not before seen in
action, and feeling childishly proud that anyone they passed
might think she was already his wife. But it had quickly become
clear that, as little beauties went, the car had an ugly side too
– and that 'for ever' was a very long time. Every five or six miles
it would shudder to a halt, refusing to be coaxed back into life
until Keith had leapt out, opened the bonnet and rapped ener-
getically on its 'springs' (whatever they might be) with a
hammer he'd obviously brought with him for the purpose. Not
that he'd explained as much when Shirley had first climbed in
and questioned why they needed it. 'You never know,' he'd told

her, his expression one of great seriousness. 'There could be bandits or anyone out on the roads to Preston. I brought it so I could protect us if we get accosted.'

So it was, then, that when she eventually dozed off, somewhere near Manchester, her dreams were plagued by mask-wearing ne'er-do-wells brandishing knives and swords and demanding what little money they had between them, as well as her mother's freshly baked Victoria sponge cake. She jumped in the darkness as she was finally jolted awake, the chilly air forming a white haze in front of her face. And was that ice on the *inside* of the windows?

'Come on, you lazy mare!' Keith was saying as he shook Shirley's shoulder. 'We're here.'

'What time is it?' she asked him, trying to stretch her frozen limbs. She felt welded to the seat. 'Blimey. I'm bloody freezing!'

'Yeah, you would be,' he told her, opening the driver's door and letting an Arctic wind in to join them. 'That's because there's no heater and it's January. This isn't a bleeding Rolls-Royce, Shirl! And it's nearly tea-time, I reckon. We passed a town-hall clock a few miles back and it was half four then. So, yep, nearly tea-time is my guess. Come on, get your skates on and let's get inside and thaw out.'

As she got out of the car and reached into the back for her small, brown leather suitcase, Shirley saw Margaret's home for the first time. Here was something for which the words 'little beauty' were the correct ones. Behind a white-painted wooden gate lay a neat little garden, bisected by a straight flagstone path. It was flanked by flowerbeds that, while resting from their summertime endeavours, were still nicely dug and punctuated by neatly pruned bushes. Shirley was completely taken aback as her gaze travelled around. She knew Margaret and Bob's lives were somewhat different from the family's back in Tamar Street, but she'd never imagined anything quite as grand as this. It looked like somewhere that you might imagine a posh family from the telly living, certainly not someone like the brash matriarch that was Annie Hudson; no wonder she'd been so keen to stop up here since Reggie had died. And, no doubt, so reluctant to return to the Canterbury estate, because this was a whole other world. Although it was quite dark now, the house positively twinkled; there was no mistaking the fact that this home, and this area, was very different to that of either Canterbury or Lidget Terrace, and she felt an unexpected stab of self-consciousness.

When Margaret came to the door to show them in, however, she felt immediately at home; there were no airs and graces here, as her own mam might have put it – even though she certainly had a few of those of her own. The house inside was as grand as the outside, with a beautiful hall carpet that ran through into the living room, and right up to the walls on all sides. The furniture was beautiful, too – light and modern, just like the furniture she and Keith had drooled over in Busby's in Bradford, and which they'd not be able to afford for years, if ever. But it wasn't just the posh furniture that made the place feel so pretty – it was all the plants; Margaret had plants in pots everywhere. On the window ledges and sideboard – even one big green plant in a giant tub on the floor. Shirley smiled appreciatively, imagining how her own little home could be. This was so nice – this was what a home *should* look like.

Shirley had only met Bob and Margaret twice before, and both occasions had been sad ones – family funerals. But even based on their short acquaintance, Shirley had formed a strong impression of Margaret. She was 42 now; not only older and more affluent as a consequence, but also a lot milder in temperament than either young Annie or June. She was also practical, and clearly now the head of the whole Hudson family. With Reggie gone, and Annie now diminished and drinking heavily, it was clearly Margaret the others called on for help and support. She'd seen it in action herself; how she'd swooped in with Bob when Reggie had died, driven that long four or five hours to Bradford and calmly sorted out all the arrangements, making everyone feel safe and reassured.

Margaret had her own son, of course, Terry – who was stopping with his gran at his Auntie Eunice's for a couple of days to free his bed up – but to Shirley's mind, she also seemed like a second mum to Keith now, and Shirley saw something in her that she saw in her own mother: someone on whom they could rely if they were ever in trouble. Someone who'd be there for them both.

She also looked delighted to see them. 'Oh, you poor things,' she said, pulling Shirley over the step to hurry her inside. 'You look chilled to the bone. Look at your cheeks, love! They're scarlet!'

The interior of the house was warm and toasty and wafting through from the kitchen came the unmistakable smell of a thick, meaty stew. Shirley drew it into her nostrils and felt her mouth water. She wasn't just cold, she was also hungry. All they'd had to eat on the long drive from Bradford was the packet of ham sandwiches Mary had made and wrapped for them, and that had been hours back, long before she'd fallen asleep. Smelling the stew now had her stomach rumbling in anticipation.

Fortunately, Margaret wasted no time in sending them off up to their rooms to unpack, with the instruction to hurry as they'd dish up right away.

'Oh, I love your house so much, Margaret,' Shirley said, once they were sitting down around the dining table with big bowls of stew. She was even more in awe now she'd been up and seen the prettily decorated bedrooms and the upstairs bathroom – which, to Shirley's wonderment, contained an actual pink bath and toilet! 'And this is gorgeous, too,' she added, pointing to her food appreciatively, as tendrils of steam rose deliciously towards her nose.

'Ta, love,' Margaret said, 'but I'm afraid I can't take the credit. Bob made the food. He might have to watch for his fingers now his eyes are going, bless him, but he's the cook in this house. Always has been. I'm worse than useless, me,' she said, laughing, 'Just ask our Terry.'

Bob had eye problems and Keith had told Shirley he'd prob-ably go blind in a few years, and she marvelled at their ability to laugh about such a horrible prospect. But that was the way the Hudsons did everything, it seemed. Rolled their sleeves up and got on with it, however difficult. It was one of the traits she admired most in them.

Bob and Keith were laughing too. 'Our Margaret could burn a pot of tea, Shirl,' he told her. 'Bob's a chef,' he explained. 'Used to be a cook in the army.'

'I was indeed,' Bob confirmed in his strange southern accent – something that had fascinated Shirley since the first time she'd met him. She'd never spoken to anyone who spoke like he did before – only heard those sorts of voices on the telly. It was a whole other world, the way people spoke to each other on the telly, and it felt peculiar to hear it in this dining room in Preston. But nice-peculiar, even so. She could listen to him all day.

He leaned towards Shirley now, as if reading her mind. 'And our Keith knows a good stew when he sees one, as well, Shirley.

You should ask him sometime about when he came to stay with us down in Kent.' He looked up at his wife and winked. 'Don't you think so, Margaret? What was it again? Coq au vin, wasn't it, Keith?'

Shirley looked from one to the other, confused by their conspiratorial looks, but then Margaret burst out laughing, and Keith groaned theatrically.

'Bob, you twat,' he said, shaking his head. 'Not *again* …'

'What?' Shirley wanted to know, now that all three were laughing. 'Am I missing something?'

'Nothing you'll want to hear, Shirl,' Keith assured her. 'Not over dinner, at any rate.'

'Yes, I do,' she replied.

'Yes, she does,' Margaret added. 'Go on, *tell* her, Keith. Can't imagine why you haven't told her already, truth be known.'

'I bleeding can,' Keith retorted. 'I still get the shivers thinking about it now.'

'Shivers? What, is it a ghost story or something?' Shirley asked him, keen to hear for herself what was clearly amusing them all so much.

'Er, not exactly,' Bob said. 'Though still haunting for you, eh, Keith?'

Which had them all bursting into great peals of laughter yet again.

'Keith, just frigging *tell* me!' she commanded.

Back when Keith had been in the army, he'd been based in the barracks at Biggin Hill in Kent and, when on leave, rather than make the long journey back up north to Bradford, he'd often stay at Bob and Margaret's house in Kent instead. This gave him a base from which he could enjoy spending his free time in London, doing a round of his favourite pubs, with or without his army mates, then just jump on a late train at Charing Cross back to where his sister lived.

This particular day, he'd been surprised to bump into an old friend from Canterbury estate. 'It was Bobby,' he explained to Shirley. 'Bobby Moran. Back then he was a bit of a drifter and he'd often do things like that, just hop on a train from Bradford and see where it took him, see if he could earn a few bob for somewhere to kip and food and beer. Then, when he'd had enough, he'd hop on a train back. Always called it "going on my jollies". Anyway, naturally, we got together, see what we could get up to for a couple of days; he was always skint –'

'Probably still is,' remarked Margaret drily.

Keith agreed. 'And you know me – never turn down an opportunity to make a few bob, eh? And it was easy enough to have a quick word with the pianist, get up and sing for the punters, with Bobby working the crowd, collecting pennies in his trilby.'

'And?' Shirley prompted, after Keith had paused for a mouthful.

'And, naturally, this being Bobby, once we'd divvied up the money, off he wanders and I'm left to get drunk on my own. So I get talking to this older guy who's been sitting watching me singing. London bloke, very posh voice. But seemed okay. Told me he was a retired sailor, and he looked the part as well – apparently spent most of his years in the navy. Anyway, I buy him a couple of pints out of my singing money, just to be sociable, and when it gets to three o'clock, I'm not ready for chucking out yet.' Keith turned to Bob now. 'You know what it's like when you've had loads to drink, don't you? You want to stay out all frigging night.'

Shirley laughed. 'Correction. *You* do, Keith. The rest of us know better. Most of us know when we've had enough.'

'Well, anyway,' Keith continued, 'with the pub shut till six, I'm at a bit of a loss as to what to do. It feels way too early to head back to Margaret and Bob's, but being on my own, I'm at a bit of a loose end. "Tell you what," says the old bloke. "I don't live far from here. How about you come back to mine for a bit of dinner. I live with my sister and she always cooks loads. Then you can head back to the pub later on." "Are you sure?" I ask. Because it feels like a bit of an imposition, obviously. But he insists and, as I'm starving, I agree. We get in his car then – he says his place is only ten minutes' drive away, and it is – and it's a lovely place, as well. Very grand. And in the garden there's this washing line, with his sister's stockings and smalls hanging from it, so I'm thinking – hmm, wonder if we're talking a younger sister, here?'

Shirley punched Keith in the arm. 'Trust you, you bleeding pervert!'

Margaret laughed. 'Oh, believe me, you ain't heard nothing yet, Shirl.'

'All right, Margaret, no need to rub it in,' Keith said, shaking his head. 'Anyway, so we go inside and straight away I can smell this lovely dinner cooking, but there's no sign of the sister. "Oh, she must have nipped out," the old man says, "but she'll have dinner on for us, don't worry. Nice chicken casserole," he goes. "Made in the French style. Coq au vin,"' he added, grimacing at Bob. '"Meanwhile," he says, taking me into this grand sitting room, "why don't we sit down and watch a bit of telly?" He then draws the curtains, shutting out the daylight – "so we can see it better," he tells me – then tells me to sit on the couch and he turns the telly on.

'And you know when you start to feel funny about something?' Keith said. 'That something's not quite right? Well, that was the feeling I got when I sat down on that couch. Still, I was starving, so though it felt weird, sitting there with him in the dark, I thought I'd probably eat the dinner before heading on my way. But then – and it was so sudden, I had no idea what was coming – he suddenly drops his pants and throws himself down on the rug!'

Shirley gaped. 'What? Oh my God – he *didn't*?'

'He bleeding *did*,' Keith said, the image obviously still a sharp and painful memory. 'Right there in front of me – trousers down like a flash, all his money falling out of his pockets and rolling round the floor – and there's worse than that, too. He's got his trousers round his ankles, now, and he's trying to kick his shoes off, and underneath he's got all this *stuff* on.'

'What stuff?' Shirley wanted to know.

'Women's stuff! Women's stockings and suspenders, lacy bleeding knickers, the lot!'

'Oh, my God!' Shirley spluttered again. 'So there wasn't any sister, then?'

Keith shrugged. 'Haven't a clue – I didn't frigging wait to find out! I just jumped up, grabbed some coins off the floor for me bus fare back to Leicester Square, kicked him right up the arse and then ran for my life!'

'I'll bet,' Shirley agreed, trying to imagine the shock of it. 'So there wasn't a sister – *he* was the sister. I've read about stuff like that.'

Bob laughed. 'Shame young Keith hadn't, eh, lad? Could have got in one heck of a sticky situation there.'

'Don't I know it?' Keith agreed. 'I found a bus going back to the West End and went back to the same pub. Never needed a shot of whisky so badly in my entire life. And *they* all knew. All the regulars – all of them were grinning at me and tittering. They knew *exactly* what had been going on. And just think about it, Shirl – he'd been sitting there in all that garb, chatting away –'

'Chatting you *up*,' Margaret corrected.

'Too right!' Keith agreed sheepishly. 'What an idiot. Let me tell you, Shirl,' he added, pinching thumb and finger together, 'I was *that* close to being *his* coq au bleeding vin! Could have put me off for life, that could.'

Shirley blushed as he winked at her. Somehow, she didn't think so.

Chapter 15

3 March 1962

Shirley stared up to the ceiling and tried to get her bearings. She could sense something was wrong, even though she couldn't quite work out what it was. She closed her eyes again, conscious that sleep could easily reclaim her, snuggled as she was under the soporific weight of sheets and blankets, and with her head cradled by the sweet-smelling feather pillow. But, no; there was definitely something prodding at her consciousness, but what? She rolled over, opening her eyes again and straightening out her legs, only to find herself nose to nose with her sleeping fiancé and – worse still – with her bare thigh hard up against the warm flesh of his.

'Keith!' she hissed, springing away from him as if she'd touched molten metal. 'Oh, my God, Keith! What time is it?'

He barely stirred – his only response was a drowsy half-smile. 'Keith!' she hissed again, wriggling upright and trying to shake him awake.

His own lashes parted only slowly. He'd been deeply asleep, clearly. Was still half asleep now. 'Wassup, Shirl?' he mumbled blearily, hauling both arms from beneath the covers and using the heels of his hands to rub his eyes awake. Then, as consciousness brought consternation, he blinked at her. 'Hang on,' he said. 'What are you doing here, anyway?'

Shirley knew he only had his underpants on under those covers, and the recollection only stressed her more. Especially in conjunction with the look in his eye when he realised she was climbing out of, rather than into, the bed. How could he have forgotten? Had he really been *that* drunk?

No, he hadn't, she thought ruefully, her cheeks colouring at the memory. 'Don't even think it!' she said, waggling a finger at him while he reached for the little alarm clock on the far bedside table. 'Keith, you don't get it. I've been here all frigging *night*!'

He raised the clock to his face and squinted at the tiny hands. 'Just gone eight,' he reassured her as he replaced it with a clatter. 'Anyway, why are you getting in such a flap? You're all right for a bit yet. It's Saturday, don't forget. And you're not due down the market till eleven. Come on. Stop fretting. Come back in the warm for another cuddle.'

He flapped the covers back and patted the space in the bed suggestively. But even the prospect of snuggling up against his lean, almost-naked body wasn't enough to quell the terror in Shirley's heart. 'Keith, how can you think about things like that at a time like this? Are you mad? Oh, shit, Keith. My dad is going to *kill* me!'

He grinned. Then let his gaze travel down to her bare legs and feet. 'Well, you know what they say, Shirl,' he said, reaching out to tug at her wrist. 'May as well be hung for a sheep as a lamb, eh? If he's going to kill you anyway, might as well make it worth it.'

Oh, to be able to. But she dithered for only a fraction of a second before grabbing the tights that lay in a muddle on the rug under her toes, a snake-like coil that only seemed to emphasise her wickedness even more. They were the very same tights that she had begged her mam to buy for her only a few days earlier. A luxury she definitely couldn't afford herself. But she'd been so desperate to get her hands on a pair. Everyone was wearing them now; they were all the rage currently – and such a blessed change from all that fiddling around with stockings and suspenders. She'd been thrilled to bits when her mum had said she'd treat her to a pair.

A pair she had promised she would look after. And obviously hadn't.

'Are you *mad*?' she yelped again as she snatched them up and began furiously bunching one leg so she could put them back on. What had she been thinking? 'I don't care about frigging work, Keith! My dad is going to go mental. I should never have stayed. And you told me you'd set that bloody alarm clock, for that matter!'

'I did!' he said indignantly, sitting up and reaching for it again.

'And he'll be up. No doubt about it,' she went on, imagining him sitting, clock-watching, waiting for her return. 'And when he realises I'm not at home … oh, God, I hope my mam's there to stick up for me.'

'See?' Keith said, looking at the back of the clock. 'I *did* set it. I … ah …' He glanced up at her guiltily. 'Seems I didn't *quite*.'

'Typical! I give you one simple thing to do and you can't even do it.'

'Aww, don't be mean, Shirl. I thought I had, honest. Come on, hop in for a quick cuddle to keep me going …'

Shirley gave up on the laddered tights and shoved them in her bag instead.

'See, you know you want to …' Keith began. 'And why shouldn't you? You're –'

'Yes, I *know*, Keith. Twenty-one and I can do as I like, as you never tire of telling me, but you know as well as I do that it doesn't matter a bit to my mam and dad. My dad, who is now going to kill me,' she added, reaching for her skirt and pulling it on.

'At least gi's a kiss before you go, then,' Keith persisted. Shirley looked over him and softened. She couldn't help it. He looked so lovely, with his hair all higgledy-piggledy, and his just-awake face, and his bare chest and shoulders all chiselled and sinewy from the hard, physical grafting he did at work all day.

'Go on, then,' she said, leaning over to do as instructed, only to have him grab her and pull her off her feet and on to the bed with him, clearly not about to take no for an answer.

But 'no' it had to be. Or even worse might happen. 'You stop that right this minute, Keith Hudson!' she said, giggling despite herself as she finally managed to wriggle from his grasp. 'Love, I really do have to go. I can almost hear the steam coming out of his ears from here. I'll have a quick cat-lick down in the kitchen and see you after work, okay?'

Keith groaned theatrically and flopped back down on the bed. 'You're a cruel, cruel woman, you are, Shirley Read! Okay then, love,' he added, rolling on to his side as she picked up her bag. 'I'll come down about half ten to give you a lift to work, shall I?'

Shirley shook her head. 'No, I'll get the bus. Best you don't come to the house this morning. I don't want him starting on you with the wedding any minute now. Don't want the pair of you falling out at this stage. Plenty of time for that *after* the wedding.'

'Good luck,' Keith said. 'And remember …'

'Yes, I *know*. I'm 21 and can do what I like.'

She felt a thrill of excitement and defiance, despite the dressing down that would probably be imminent. In a week it would finally be true – she could do what she liked.

Shirley ran down the cold stone steps, shivering as her feet made contact with the treads, and made a mental note to talk to Keith about getting a carpet one day for the stairs. It would be so nice to have them carpeted, like Reggie and Vera. They were the talk of the street, what with being so posh.

She needed a wee pretty desperately but there was no way she'd have gone in the bucket Keith kept beside the bed – she'd blanch at the very thought, in fact. There were some things a lady just didn't do. But neither could she risk going to the outhouses. She was afraid she might bump into someone she knew. Not her mam and dad – their end of Lidget Terrace was served by a different block of toilets – but the chances of seeing someone she *didn't* know were tiny, and with the speed such news travelled it would be all about in no time – precisely the thing that would most infuriate her father and give her mother an attack of the vapours.

No, she'd hang on, she thought, reaching for one of their still brand-new tea towels and turning the tap on, doing the universal hip-jiggling 'save it till later' dance that all women know how to do.

Once the tea towel was moistened sufficiently to scrub her shameful face, she stared out onto the cobbled street. How on earth had Keith talked her into staying the night? And *there*, of all places? She knew her dad might have forgiven it if they'd been going to someone else's and he could have been reassured they'd been staying in separate bedrooms, like they had when they'd visited Margaret and Bob. But they'd been alone, and he'd guess that – Shirley couldn't lie to her dad about it, either.

She'd done wrong and was just going to have to face the music. Which brought a smile to her lips as she checked she looked respectable. Yes. Perhaps she should just blame it on the music.

Not that the night had begun with any dishonourable intentions. They'd gone out the previous evening to the Black Bull at Little Horton, for a bit of a pre-wedding celebration. It was also a chance to have a proper Hudson get-together, now that Margaret and Bob had come down. They were staying with Reggie and Vera and their boys, while Keith's mam stayed at Annie's and, along with Malcolm, who Keith had asked to be his best man, and his wife Val, who was one of the bridesmaids, they'd all been in the mood for a bit of a shindig.

It had turned into a great night, with family members popping up all over the place and, as was usually the case, the drink flowed freely. Young Annie and Keith had been up singing, entertaining the whole pub, and, halfway through the evening, even their Charlie had turned up – and promptly gone and ordered drinks all round, despite not having a penny with which to pay for them. But, Charlie being Charlie, nothing was said about this detail; perhaps, Shirley reasoned, they were doing such goodness anyway that one free round among so many didn't much matter.

It turned out there were many, many rounds. The pub stayed open till very late in order to accommodate their happy customers, and when Keith and Shirley arrived back at Lidget Terrace a little after two o'clock in the morning, she did feel extremely happy – and definitely not in the mood to go home yet, despite the wobbly half-hour walk home.

She had to be honest with herself. It had taken almost nothing for Keith to persuade her to sneak into number 17 and be alone together for a bit in the home that in just over a week

would be *their* home – the home where they'd finally consum-
mate their marriage and hopefully start the family she so
craved.

But that week made the difference – the fundamental difference – and she agreed only on the basis that there'd be no
funny business, and that they'd set the alarm to go off at 8 a.m.
sharp so she could sneak home before her parents woke up.
That way, she'd reasoned with her late-night fuzzy logic, it
would be almost like coming in 'extremely late', as opposed to
rolling in the following morning.

'But come on, Shirl,' Keith had pleaded when they got in,
both tiddly and giggling. 'You're not going to make me sleep on
the couch, are you? I put the record player up in the bedroom
earlier, so we can put that on and just have a cuddle. I swear on
my life I won't try anything on.'

He'd crossed himself theatrically, in order to demonstrate
his sincerity, and, since she found it hard to resist him at the
best of times, she eventually conceded, even though she was
well aware that it was the same lack of willpower where Keith's
charms were concerned that was likely to be her undoing.

'But I'm not taking all my clothes off,' she said as she headed
unsteadily up the stairs. 'I'll be keeping my underskirt and
tights on.'

Keith laughed at this as he followed, lending a supporting
hand to her backside. 'Yes, ma'am,' he said, caressing her.
'Anything you say, ma'am.'

'I mean it, Keith,' she said, trying to sound sterner than she
was feeling. 'You promised we'd wait till after we were married.
So I mean it – no funny business, okay?'

* * *

Once in the bedroom, Keith switched on the light before going across to draw the curtains, prompting Shirley, who still had at least some of her wits about her, to go across and turn the light off again. However bold she was in some ways, she was extremely shy about her body, and the thought of Keith seeing her taking her clothes off – even if only half of them – was unthinkable.

'Hey, Shirl,' he protested, 'how am I supposed to see to put a record on?'

'If you open those curtains again, you'll manage well enough from the moonlight,' she replied, undressing herself as far as she thought was appropriate under the circumstances, while he did so. She then slipped quickly into the cold bed and wriggled her legs around to try to make it warmer, while Keith took off all but his underpants with great enthusiasm, whipping his trousers off, leg by leg, and flinging them into a far corner, mindless of how much they'd crease. Shirley smiled to herself. She'd have to nag him about things like that at some point. But not now. Tonight she found it rather lovely.

'Aren't you cold?' she asked, as she watched him first set the alarm clock then find a record and place it on the turntable. She noticed with a rush of affection that he was already dancing – well, after a fashion, anyway – to a tune that must be running inside his head. Shirley marvelled at seeing him so unselfconsciously nearly naked; marvelled at the thought that in just over a week from tonight, they'd be in this very bedroom, the long wait finally over, free to be with each other as husband and wife finally, able to dispense with the shackles of underskirts and tights. The thought of being naked with him thrilled and frightened her in roughly equal measure. He would finally see – finally *have* – all of her.

'Ta da!' he announced suddenly, and the air was full of sound. Unexpected sound, too; she'd thought he'd choose some sort of love song or ballad – but he'd put on the *William Tell* Overture. It was one of her favourite pieces of music, and it meant a lot to both of them because it was the first record that she and Keith had bought together.

Young Annie was a great fan of classical music and she'd had a version by someone called Rossini. 'You're a pair of reprobates,' she'd joked when they'd bought their own copy and it had turned out to be a rock and roll version by the Ventures. She'd gone one further when Keith confessed he loved it because it was the theme tune to *The Lone Ranger*, and roundly clipped him round the head for being so common.

But that was the truth of it, and who cared why they liked it anyway? Keith turned around then and, with a whoop, mimed the Lone Ranger riding an imaginary horse towards the bed, making her burst out laughing as he jumped in beside her, went 'brrrr!' and quickly enfolded her in his arms.

'You silly get!' she began, but the words were soon derailed by the much more pressing business of kissing and cuddling, which, now they were in the place they both most wanted to be, was gathering momentum along with the music.

Within minutes, Shirley found herself pinned under her ardent fiancé and most definitely not wanting to shove him away. Thank God she'd insisted on keeping her tights on, she thought distractedly, because she knew the way she was feeling meant that if the unthinkable started happening, she'd be too swept away to stop herself letting it. As it was, she found herself in the bizarre situation of being made love to, but not – not to mention feeling the stretched nylon pulling at her toes in time to the crescendo of drums and trumpets.

Keith rolled off her finally, clearly spent and sighing happily. And as she tingled with excitement and felt her pulse slowing down, she wondered – did this mean she was no longer a virgin? She turned on her side to ask Keith but, as she'd already half suspected, he was flat on his back, spark out and snoring. *No*, she told herself sternly, as she watched his chest rise and fall. She still had her tights and pants on. So she *couldn't* be. But as she wriggled the tights off – she'd popped a toe through both feet now, annoyingly – she still felt her cheeks begin to burn.

Shirley's cheeks were still burning now, and it wasn't from the cold air, as she'd made the short journey from one house to the other. Her dad was sitting in his usual spot by the fire, just as she'd expected, and his expression told her all she needed to know. That there was probably no point in trying to explain herself. She would try anyway, she decided.

'Dad, I'm sorry,' she said. 'It just got so late. And I'd had a bit to drink – we were all out celebrating for the wedding and, well …' She stopped, not knowing what else to say, braced for him to tear her off a strip.

Raymond was staring at her, his eyes boring into her soul, it seemed, and what upset her all the more was that it wasn't the expected anger on his face that she saw – it was disappointment. Deep disappointment.

'Get out of my sight, Shirley,' he said, his voice as quiet as her own had been. 'The celebrating generally comes *after* the wedding. *All* the celebrating,' he finished, turning his face away, dismissing her, as if he couldn't bear to look at her. His only gesture was to her mam, who'd been standing silently in the doorway, to go across and turn the television on for him.

Shirley hung her head. The way he'd looked at her, there was no point in arguing with him. No point in pointing out that, just as Keith had kept saying, she *was* a grown woman. One who'd be living with her husband in that same house in a week. She had broken the rules and that was all there was to it. She'd let him down. She'd done wrong. She'd disappointed him.

It was that more than anything that brought the lump to her throat; that and the fact that she'd only had about two hours sleep, off the back of which she'd now have to wash and change and go to work.

She did as she'd been told and went into the kitchen, thirsty and, despite the lump in her throat, ravenous as well. She reached for the kettle. She needed tea and perhaps a slice of toast. Mary followed her. 'Oh, Mam, he's in a right mood with me,' Shirley said, sobbing, as her mam gathered her into her arms to give her a cuddle. 'I didn't mean to stay all night, honest I didn't. And I swear on my life, we didn't do anything. We really didn't, Mam.'

'Hush, love,' Mary soothed. 'Take no notice of your dad. He'll be all right. It'll all be forgotten by the time you get wed, you'll see. Why don't you go upstairs and have a long soak and sort that pretty face out? You've time enough still, haven't you? I'll get some breakfast ready for you once you're done.'

Grateful for her mother at least, Shirley mounted the stairs slowly, her feet feeling leaden, the lack of sleep already beginning to make its presence felt. Worse than that, though, was the leaden feeling that had lodged in her heart as well since seeing the way her father had looked at her. It would have been better if he *had* shouted, she decided. Much better. She could have argued back. Instead, what she now felt was dirty, like she'd let him down badly. Like he was ashamed of her. All that waiting and being sensible and doing things properly, and one frigging alarm clock had undone it all. Or, rather, Keith had, by not setting it properly. Yes, her mam was probably right – it would all be forgotten by this time next week, but the thought of her dad's disgusted expression remaining in place made next Saturday seem a long way away now.

She had a bath and dressed in her work clothes, her mood as glum and dark now as it had been giggly and light only a few hours before. She'd made her bed and she'd have to lie in it – there was nothing else for it – but she really didn't feel in the mood for a day down the market, and the thought of Keith enjoying a lie-in just up the road – in *their* marital bed – made her even more irritable. And when she pulled the tights from her bag – fit for nothing but the bin now – the ruination of her day was complete.

Not quite, as it turned out. Because as soon as she came back down – taking care not to so much as glance into the sitting room – she realised she'd left both her warm gloves and her apron up at the new house, having gone there straight from work the previous Saturday. So she'd have to run back up and get them, which meant she'd probably miss the bus. She felt tears spring in her eyes again, but by an effort of will managed to stem them, brushing the back of her hand across her eyes as she shot through the door, hoping her luck would change and the bus would be late.

She ran up the road, into the house and straight into the arms of Keith, who'd been heading out just as she was heading in. He grinned and lifted his hands up – her apron was in one, and her gloves were in the other. She could have kissed him.

'I was just about to drive down to take you to work,' he said. 'Thought I'd do the honourable thing and brave the wrath of Gunga Din.' He winked at her suggestively. 'Seemed only fair under the circumstances.'

This had Shirley's cheeks burning in shame again, which was annoying it itself. Why was it all right for lads but not for girls? Why were there so many rules about what girls were allowed to do, when the lads – or so it seemed to her – could do anything they liked?

But her fractious mood was dispelled only half an hour later. Once Keith had dropped her off and she'd gone to put the first of her gloves on, she felt something crinkle inside. It was a piece of paper, folded twice, and as she opened it up she knew what she'd find – one of his little poems.

And she wasn't disappointed. He'd written:

> I know I can be stupid, and I know I drive you mad,
>   And I'm not the best looking Canterbury lad,
>   But I want you to know, my beautiful Shirl,
>   That, without a doubt, you're my kinda girl,
>   So though I know today that you're feeling bleak,
>   Just think, it's Mrs Hudson from next week!

Chapter 16

10 March 1962

'June! Bloody hurry up!' Mary yelled into the kitchen from the living room. It was 7:30 a.m. on the day of the wedding, and Shirley was sitting patiently in her corset and underskirt on the wooden chair at the back of the room. She felt happy to be up early, as she'd hardly slept a wink. And there was lots to be done, in any case, as they were getting married at 11 o'clock, but her Auntie June wanted a ciggie break – which she'd have to take on the doorstep – and to put the kettle on for a second cup of tea. And what Auntie June wanted, she generally got.

'I won't be a minute now!' she called irritably back at her older sister. 'Stop bloody bossing everyone about, will you? We've got hours yet!'

Shirley loved her Auntie June. The youngest of her mam's two sisters, she was only five years older than Shirley, and knew everything about everything – well, all the important things, anyway, in much the same way Keith's sisters Annie and June did as well. She knew about hairstyles and fashion and how to make your make-up look fabulous, so it was no wonder it was June that everyone wanted to do their hair and make-up, and Shirley couldn't wait to see her transformation complete.

It was no secret in the family that Mary resented June's youth and good looks. In fact, Shirley's mam being Shirley's mam, she rarely invited her round to the house for fear that Raymond might look at her for too long, or in the wrong way. It was perhaps also one of the reasons why, when June *did* come to visit, her dad almost always disappeared.

Whatever the ins and outs of it, it all felt a bit unfair to Shirley's mind, because she wished she could see more of her glamorous young auntie, who generally sneaked round when her mum wasn't around. Still, now she was going to have her own place, perhaps she would.

'It's okay, Mam,' Shirley said. 'You can go see to yourself now if you like. Auntie June won't take much longer, and I'm almost done, I think.'

Mary studied Shirley's half-pinned-up hair and still naked face with a distinctly pained expression. She'd been checking the time at five-minute intervals since they'd got up, flapping so much it was almost as if she was getting married herself. She shook her head. 'No, love, I need to know you're all sorted out first. I'll just wait till eight, then I'll go upstairs and help sort your dad out. You know what our June's like – she'll go off the boil; she's a bit slack if I'm not watching over her.'

'Mam, I'm *fine*,' Shirley began reassuring her.

'Yes, she's *fine*,' June repeated, grinning as both Mary and Shirley turned to see her standing there in the doorway, ciggies and lighter in one hand, cup of tea in the other, obviously having heard what her sister had just said. She winked at Shirley. 'Go on, Mary, go and sort Raymond out – I've left some tea mashing in the pot for him, if you want to take him up a cup, by the way.' She placed her own cup down on the window-sill and threw the packet of cigarettes back into her handbag. 'Right, then. Let's get our beautiful Cinders ready for her ball, shall we?'

Mary looked on disapprovingly, fanning her face as if she could still smell the cigarette smoke on her sister, 'Oh, that won't be any good, June,' she sniffed. 'He only likes it the way *I* do it. Not bloody stewed for half an hour like you do!' And with that pronouncement made, she then flounced off into the kitchen – a blur of floral dressing gown and giant rollers – and started banging around in what Shirley knew was a very pointed fashion. Among June's various crimes – which were heinous and numbered several, according to Mary – one was that she was a lazy housewife, who didn't clean her house properly, as a woman should, so whenever June was round, she always made a big thing of scrubbing the kitchen down, whether it needed it or not.

'There she goes,' June whispered into Shirley's ear now. 'Hankering after being a pin-up girl for Vim again!'

Shirley giggled at the mental image. 'Stop it, June!' she whispered. 'You know what she'll be like if she hears you saying that! Come on. Stop making me laugh and start making me gorgeous.'

But June wasn't to be side-tracked. Checking the doorway, she grabbed hold of the hairbrush she'd just been using and, flicking it like a feather duster, started waltzing round the living room, doing a perfect rendition of a scene in *Calamity Jane*.

'A *woman's touch* ...' she began trilling, '*can quickly fill ... the empty flower glasses on the winder-sill ...*'

'I can HEAR you!' snapped Mary, from beyond the door.

By the time it was ten o'clock, Shirley was almost ready, and when she was finally allowed to see herself in the mirror, she gasped in surprise at her reflection. She felt the prettiest she'd ever felt in her life. Her dark hair had been beautifully curled and pinned into place, and adorned with a sparkling diamante tiara. Her make-up was flawless, her skin fair and dewy, and her lips shined with the Vaseline June had put on over her carefully chosen pale-pink lipstick. All that remained was for Mary and June to help her into the dress that her mam had said cost a week's wages, but which Shirley knew she'd been paying for in instalments for three months. For all her plans to make her own dress, rather than waste pots of money, Shirley couldn't have been more thrilled when her mam told her they'd be buying one for her. It had been fitted especially for her in Bridge Street Bridal Boutique, and was the most gorgeous thing she'd ever had. It had hung ready in her bedroom for a few days now, a shimmering, magical presence, and Shirley couldn't wait to step into it and complete the transformation.

Shirley thought of Keith then. Was he as excited as she was? Was he nervous? Was he *ready*? She felt her stomach flip – both at the thought of him seeing her in her wedding dress, and at the thought of him finding the whole thing too much and of doubts perhaps creeping in and scaring him. It was such a big thing, to be married, after all.

The week had crawled by, as Shirley had always known it would. But with one highlight – the fact that she and Keith were able to enjoy a rare day off with two of the most important people at the wedding. Annie's little daughter, Linda, was going to be a flower girl and her Auntie June's son Tony the page boy. They were both six, and Shirley and Keith babysat them individually often, but as soon as they clapped eyes on one another – when round at Shirley's mam's, trying on their outfits, several weeks back – they'd immediately become inseparable, so were thrilled to bits when Keith suggested they take them off their respective mams' hands for a bit and go for an outing to a well-known local beauty spot called Shipley Glen.

They were an odd match – chalk and cheese, in many ways; Tony, a quiet, well-mannered lad, friendly but very reserved, and Linda, every bit as confident and outspoken as everyone else in her enormous family – and no wonder, having Annie for a mum. She also shared Annie's good looks and, with her huge eyes and chocolate ringlets, always looked as pretty as a picture. All in all she looked as if butter wouldn't melt in her mouth, which wasn't necessarily the case.

It was still early in the season, but Shipley Glen was always busy, and when they'd had their picnic and an ice cream – even though it was fairly chilly – they joined a big throng strolling over the bridge that led down to the river. They were almost there – and a long way from any public conveniences – when Tony announced that he needed the toilet.

'Just go over there behind that tree,' Keith had told him. 'Lots of boys have a wee in the woods.'

'But I don't want a wee, Uncle Keith,' Tony whispered. 'I need a number two. An' I need it *now*!' finished the now rather anguished little boy.

Keith rolled his eyes, but Shirley managed to find some scraps of tissue for them and Keith duly trotted off with Tony, deep as he could into the patch of trees nearby.

'Yuck!' announced a disgusted Linda. 'That's revolting, Auntie Shirley!' Upon which Shirley explained that sometimes you had to do what you had to do and that it was either that or a very, very long and possibly urgent walk back.

And she'd thought that was the last of it, as well. Keith and Tony returned, the latter looking mightily relieved, and they continued on over the bridge to look at the ducks on the river. Shirley was getting used to the admiring glances of people when they were out with the children, as both were invariably immaculately dressed by their mothers, and equally sweet and well behaved. Today, however, Linda noticed an elderly gentle-man walking with his wife, and as he pointed towards them, asked 'What's that old man looking at, Auntie Shirley?' in a voice that could have probably stopped traffic.

It was certainly loud enough that the couple stopped in their tracks.

'I think he's probably just commenting on how pretty you look,' Shirley said, trying to steer her attention back to the water. 'That and what good, well-behaved children you and Tony are.'

But there was no stopping Linda when she had a point to make, any more than there ever was with her mam. Turning to the man and his wife, who were now looking indulgently at her, she said, 'I am. I *always* am, but *he's* not a good boy. He's a mucky little tyke,' she said, pointing at a mortified Tony. 'He's just had a shit in the *woods*!'

The four of them hurried off then, and it was all Shirley and Keith could do not to burst out laughing, even while chastising Linda at the same time.

'You can't say things like that, Linda!' Keith told her, once they were well out of earshot and the prospect of poor Tony being humiliated any further.

'Why not?' Linda wanted to now. 'If he can do it, then why can't I say it?'

The answer to which would have taken some time to explain. 'You know what?' Shirley said, once they'd moved on to the play-ground and Keith and she were perched on a bench while the children played. 'I can't wait till we've got little ones of our own.'

Keith laughed. 'What, so you can teach them as many swear words as our Annie's taught her little ones?'

'No, you daft get,' she said grinning. 'So we can have fun like *this*.'

'We will, then.'

'Will what?'

'Crack on and have some, Mrs Hudson.'

'What, now? What, straight away? Oh, I'd love that *so* much. But can we? Keith, I'm not sure we can afford it.'

He pondered a moment, silently counting something on his fingers.

'*What?*' she said.

He finished counting. 'Nope,' he said, grinning back at her. 'Tried my best but as far as I can see, there's not a single member of my family who's ever let a little detail like that hold them up.' He took her hand and squeezed it. 'And I've turned out all right, haven't I?'

Shirley's dad came down the stairs just as she was about to go up, and she gasped at seeing how handsome he looked in his wedding finery. She'd seen him dressed up before, of course, for other weddings, christenings and funerals, but today he looked especially handsome and smart, which tickled Shirley, given that he'd spent most of her and Keith's courtship going on as if it was the worst thing in the world. No, today he looked, well … like he was proud to be a part of it. Suited and booted, proud and happy to be giving away his only daughter, with his hair all sleek and shiny, and the white carnation they'd fetched from the florist's yesterday, along with the rest of the flowers and her beautiful rose bouquet, already fixed to his lapel.

Her mam, too, looked a picture, in her peach-coloured two-piece, finished off with a pair of dainty matching court shoes. Shirley looked at them enviously, having wanted to wear heels for her wedding day but, as it would have made her taller than Keith, she'd chosen ivory pumps instead. And she'd been glad to. It had been the right thing to do.

'Oh, Mam and Dad,' she said, feeling the enormity of the occasion threaten to overwhelm her. 'You've done me so proud. You look just like the royal family, honest you do.'

'Stop that, lass,' Raymond said, stepping aside to prevent Shirley from flinging her arms around him. 'You'll spoil your hair, and crush my bloody flower! Go on with you – go get that wedding dress on, so we can have a good look at you afore anyone else does.'

The sleek black car that was to take Shirley to St John's Church for her wedding had been hired by Margaret and Bob as one of their wedding gifts, and trimmed with white ribbon and bows. If climbing into it on Lidget Terrace had been exciting, with all the neighbours looking on, climbing out of it, taking her father's hand as she stepped carefully onto the pavement, felt incredible.

Though it was already just gone 11 – the time they'd booked the wedding – Raymond was clearly not as keen as she was to glide straight through the church gates. 'Now, Shirley,' he said, linking arms with her and holding her still momentarily, 'I want you to know something important.' His tone was serious and when she turned to look at him, she saw his expression was as well. He cleared his throat. 'I want you to know that it isn't too late to change your mind,' he said quietly. He was now holding her gaze as well as her arm. 'If you've had second thoughts,' he went on, 'then now is the time to tell me. If you don't want to do this, just say, and I can sort it all out.'

Shirley looked at her dad, feeling the love shining in his eyes. And she knew, then and there, that everything was indeed going to be all right. That he wasn't being mean. Wasn't trying to make her change her mind. Just expressing his love in the most important way possible. Letting her know that her happiness was the thing that mattered most in his life. And if that meant calling the wedding off, he was ready to.

She wanted to throw her arms around him all over again, but, mindful of the veil that was now fixed carefully to the tiara in her hair – not to mention his carnation – merely squeezed his arm closer to her and smiled. 'I'm sure, Dad. I've never been surer of anything. I promise you, this is exactly what I want.'

Raymond smiled too, the small hint of tension leaving his eyes. He then turned to look ahead, to the church doorway. 'Well let's get you down that aisle then, lass, eh? I think you've kept young Keith waiting long enough, don't you?'

And Shirley was happier than ever not to keep her fiancé waiting any more – her fiancé, who less than an hour from now would be her husband, for better or for worse. And as the bridesmaids fell into step behind them – little Linda holding a posy of roses, to match her own, and with little Tony alongside her, bearing the red velvet cushion for the rings – she had eyes for him only. She could hear the wedding march, the swish of her train, the appreciative gasps from all the guests – but not see anything but the man she was about to wed.

He was nervous; that much had been obvious immediately, and looked no less so when she drew level and joined him. Nervous, but at the same time, a man, not a lad – strong-jawed, and filling out his smart new wedding suit. There was just the one thing. There was a very strange smell in the church, which hit her even more once she lifted her veil; a smell that put her in mind of hospitals – one that felt immediately familiar. Perhaps something they used to clean the church.

But this was no place to start sniffing and asking questions, obviously, so she did her best to ignore it as the vicar started speaking and, as the ceremony went on, she was fully occupied anyway, with all the singing and praying and saying I do-ing that the occasion demanded. All of which went by in short order and in a blur. It seemed as if almost no time had passed, or very little, before she was once again outside, about to climb into the car she'd just climbed out of, only this time while trying to shake rice and confetti from her hair – and on the arm of her husband instead of her father.

The journey from the church to the Gatehouse Club, where they were holding their reception, was only short, and something of a blur as well. They'd looked at one another, slightly stupefied, giggling like the children they suddenly felt at the reality of what had happened – at calling each other 'my husband' and 'my wife' when in public, which suddenly felt like the funniest-sounding thing in the world.

'I don't think I'll be able to, not without bursting out laughing,' Shirley confessed.

'Me neither,' Keith agreed. 'Oh, and this is mah wife, don't you know? Mrs Shirley 'udson.'

'Shirley Hudson,' she repeated, struck by the fact that, however many times she'd said it to herself, or practised writing it, pound to a penny she'd be blushing beetroot when she had to say it for real.

'How does it *feel*, though?' Keith wanted to know, once they'd clambered out and were headed for the reception hall to receive their guests. 'You know – how does it feel knowing you're now one of the Hudsons? Think you're ready for it?'

Malcolm joined them, then, linking his arm through Shirley's free one. 'Yeah – how does it feel to be my big sister, eh?'

It felt great, Shirley decided. Great, bordering on brilliant. To have siblings she could call her own, where once she'd had none. Though she wasn't allowing him that much. Not just yet. 'I don't feel any different, really,' she lied. Then, catching another whiff of the smell she'd noticed earlier, 'Oh, but did either of you smell that funny smell up by the altar, by any chance?'

Even from her position between the two of them she could half-see the change. Catch Keith's cheeks reddening as she turned to look at him, catch the warning glance he shot his brother. Definitely catch Malcolm's evident amusement at something of which she wasn't a part.

Not yet, anyway. 'Come on,' she said, stopping on the path. 'What's going on here?' She grinned. She couldn't help it. They looked just like a pair of naughty schoolboys. 'Come on,' she said again. 'We're going nowhere till you tell me what's so funny. And what that smell was, for that matter. You know, don't you?'

'Dettol,' Keith admitted, clearly knowing he was beaten.

'Dettol?' Shirley said. 'Why on earth could I smell Dettol?' She felt suddenly concerned then. She knew all about stag nights. And she knew about the Hudson brothers, as well. 'Keith,' she asked anxiously, 'are you hurt?'

Malcolm burst out laughing then. So his brother obviously wasn't. 'No,' he said, 'It's not Keith that's hurt – it was his suit that took the battering. He –'

'*Keith*!' Shirley snapped, trying hard to be cross with him. 'You promised me on your life that you wouldn't go out in that frigging suit!'

Malcolm laughed even harder. 'You'll have to take him in hand, Shirl – he didn't only go out in it. He bleeding slept in it, too! Woke up in it this morning, on the couch, and it looked like a dish rag – all wrinkled and stinking and beer-splattered, and probably worse … and, if I say so myself, I think we did a pretty good job in cleaning it up and making it look half-respectable, don't you? Sponged it off – I even found the iron and pressed it for him, too. You know,' he added proudly, 'as a proper best man should.'

'With *Dettol*?' Shirley said, shaking her head, not knowing what else to say.

'It was all we could find,' Keith explained. 'You're not going to go ballistic on me, are you, Shirl? Not today of all days? I got here, didn't I?'

'He did do that, at least,' Malcolm added. 'Come on. Could have been soooo much worse, couldn't it, Shirl?'

And might well be, at some point in the future, she mused. Her new husband was, after all, a Hudson.

But that was fine, she decided, as the three of them headed towards their waiting guests. Because she was a Hudson now, too.

Chapter 17

14 December 1962

Exactly nine months and four days after joining the ever-growing band of Mrs Hudsons, Shirley felt the first uncomfortable signs of early labour. It was an ordinary day. A day that had started like any other – well, like any other in the last few uncomfortable weeks, anyway – with her hauling her huge belly out of bed and struggling to wriggle her swollen feet into her slippers, then going down to make Keith a cup of tea before waking him up for work. But today something wasn't right; there was a niggle low down in her stomach that felt different from all the niggles she'd felt up to now. And as she stood filling the kettle for the stove, she smiled to herself, despite the discomfort. Perhaps it was happening at last.

But the smile was soon wiped off her face. No sooner had the thought come to her mind than a pain suddenly gripped her that was so unexpected it not only turned her grin into a grimace, but almost made her collapse then and there on the kitchen floor.

'Keith!' she yelled, as she staggered back out into the hallway. 'Keith, wake up! I think it's the baby!'

* * *

The thought that she might have conceived a child on her wedding night had been one that had never been far from Shirley's mind. And finding out that she was indeed pregnant, just as May had become June, had been such a blessing, despite the fact that she'd only realised because she felt so sick and ill that she was beginning to find it difficult to get out of bed in the morning. And as it showed no signs of stopping, despite the pills her doctor had given her to help with it, as blessings went, it had been mixed, to say the least.

She'd been so grateful to her parents in that regard. Though she didn't doubt they'd have treated their pregnant daughter like a princess in any event, her weakness made them insist that she give up work very early on, supporting both her and Keith – who still had to work all hours, of course – so she could stay at home and get all the rest she could.

It hadn't seemed fair. The sickness had carried on right through the pregnancy, causing her to have to bite her tongue as new mother after new mother reassured her that it would 'stop before she knew it'. Well, it hadn't! And she was also sick of hearing from other mothers about how the sicker you were, the stronger the baby was going to be.

But she tried not to dwell on the irritations of being so sickly, and instead concentrated on their amazing good fortune. With their finances so dire, Mary and Raymond had been life savers in so many ways; while the Hudsons had long since grown bored of the arrival of yet another baby into the family, for Shirley's mum and dad it was the most exciting thing ever, and they'd gone completely overboard. They bought absolutely everything anyone could think of that might be needed: the pram, the crib, the first set of clothes, packs of terry towelling nappies, stockpiles of bootees and mittens – even a special fluffy baby towel for when they bathed it. Mary and Granny

Wiggins had also spent weeks knitting tiny little woollen jackets in pure white wool, together with one or two lemon ones, for variety. 'These'll do for a girl or a boy,' Granny had assured them as she added daily to the ever-growing stack.

Several people had asked, but Shirley didn't care whether she had a baby boy or a girl. Just as long as it was healthy, that was all that really mattered. And when she wasn't feeling terrible she was in a bubble of pure happiness, feeling so much love coming from everyone that she thought she might burst.

She was particularly thrilled that the baby's due date was close to two things that mattered: Christmas and Keith's twenty-fifth birthday. And her mum and dad's financial help meant she could do something really special; rather than spend what little they did have on nappies and other essentials for the baby, she could instead make Keith's birthday extra-special by giving him a Christmas the like of which he'd never had before, including his first ever Christmas tree. Only a 3-foot artificial tree that sat perfectly on the top of their television, but by the time she'd finished adorning it with red sparkly baubles and silver tinsel, it looked spectacular, Shirley thought.

She'd probably gone a little overboard, she mused as she clutched her belly, aware of the resiny smell that was sharp in her nostrils, and of the completely over-the-top Christmas grotto she'd created in her tiny living room only two days before. There was nothing left untrimmed and no part of the downstairs had escaped her attentions with tinsel and bauble, paper chain and holly sprig, right down to the mistletoe she'd hung above the living room door.

And it had been worth it, every bit of it, just for the look on Keith's face when he'd come in from work and seen it. That and the way that he was too choked up to speak when he'd tried to. Just for the fact that by the time Christmas came around, God willing, there would be three of them to celebrate. She'd have her own little family at last.

But the grotto in the living room was now the last thing on her mind, as the niggle turned into a band of pure pain that seemed to grip her around the tummy like a giant fist. Stunned at the intensity of what she was now sure must have been a contraction, Shirley gripped the bannister and sat down heavily on the bottom step to wait for Keith to appear. It wasn't the best timing, she mused, as the pain ebbed a little. He'd been out to the Albion, up in the village, having a drink with their Malcolm the previous evening, so she knew he probably wouldn't be in the best of moods.

She eased herself back against the cool of the wall. He was also taking his time coming down. 'Keith!' she called again, and though she was at least partially reassured by the sound of his answering grunt, she wondered if she shouldn't try to make it up the street to her mam or Granny Wiggins's. Perhaps that would be the best thing to do in any case. For all the experience Keith had had dealing with babies over the years, this was women's business really, and she thought she might feel a great deal more calm and capable with someone who actually understood what she was going through by her side, holding her hand.

But looking down at her nightie decided it. Even if she could find the strength to haul herself up and out – which she was beginning to doubt – she couldn't possibly leave the house 'dressed' in such a thing. It was a hideous long affair, in a very sickly shade of pink – a virtual tent that her granny had given her as she'd grown bigger, and it made her look every bit the lumbering old lady that she currently felt. '*Keith!*' she called again, fearful that another contraction might be coming. Though she was relieved to hear the tell-tale sound of him peeing in the bedside bucket, she was also becoming scared. There was much that she didn't know but she was sure things weren't supposed to be like this. Shouldn't there be gaps between contractions, during which she'd feel perfectly fine? Wasn't that what the midwife from the clinic had told her? That she should time them and keep an eye on when the gaps started getting shorter? Things weren't making sense to her. She was sure the pain she'd felt had been a contraction, but it hadn't gone – far from it. And now it was building up again.

'Bloody hurry up!' she yelled as another horrendous pain ripped through her thighs and belly. 'Help, Keith, I think I'm dying,' she wailed, tears beginning to spill down her face. If this was just the start, how was she ever going to cope with it all?

Keith rattled down the stairs, doing his belt up as he did so. 'All right, all right!' he said, in a voice that suggested she was fussing about nothing. But then he saw her expression. 'What's up?' he asked, looking a little more concerned now. 'Shall I go get your mam to come down?'

Shirley could only nod, such was the pain – it seemed to have overtaken her entire body. And she had a sudden desperate need to lie down. Not in the stairway, however. No, she needed to lie on the cool of the kitchen lino. She managed to slither off the bottom step and crawl the short distance on all fours. She then curled up on the kitchen floor, groaning and sobbing. 'Yes, go get me mam,' she gasped, 'but hurry up, Keith, *please*. I'm frightened. I don't know what's happening to me.'

Keith's response was matter of fact. 'You're having a bloody baby, Shirl, that's all,' he informed her airily. 'I've seen my mother have a few and that's all it is, love, honest. It's the same for all women. Nothing to worry about. All be over soon.'

He stepped round Shirley then and she watched in astonishment as he reached for the piece of mirror and comb he kept in one of the kitchen cupboards.

'Frig your bleeding hair!' she yelled, wishing she had the strength to get up and bop him. 'Go get me mam! I'm *dying*, Keith!'

Men, she thought wretchedly. But he obviously didn't need telling twice.

What had possessed her? That was the thought that kept coming back to Shirley as, alone now, she tried to get back up. Why had she been in such a ridiculous hurry to start having babies? And why hadn't anyone told her it would hurt quite this much? Cursing the world and his wife, and herself for good measure, she managed to get onto hands and knees on the lino, her belly hanging low and heavy and almost touching the floor. She wasn't just in agony, she was terrified, she realised, and the thought of what was to come made fresh tears pour down her cheeks. She gripped the edge of the sink, trying to pull herself upright, and as she did so there was further cause for anxiety – not to mention humiliation – as warm liquid began pouring down the insides of her legs. Had she peed without realising? *No*, the thought rushed into her brain. It wouldn't be pee. Her waters must have broken, that would be it.

Breathing deeply to try to regain some sort of control over the searing pain, she stood still a moment, head hanging over the enamel sink, looking down into the depths of the water covering last night's dinner plates and seeing her anguished face looking back up at her. Where was Keith? What was keeping him? He should be back with her mam by now, shouldn't he? She stood up straighter, stretching out her lower back, which was beginning to hurt, too. And it was then, looking down, that she saw it. There was no pool of water on the floor as she'd expected – it was a lake of blood, bright and terrifying, lapping at her slippers and forming a bloom of scarlet against the pale pink of the nightie. She started to scream then, and collapsed back onto the floor.

Shirley had no idea how much time passed before she heard her mam's reassuring voice. It could have been moments or minutes; the pain was now so intense that she couldn't seem to think straight, the sight of the blood the only thing in her head.

'Oh, Shirley, lass,' Mary cried as she ran over to her. 'Oh, my poor girl. But don't you worry. I'm here now. Keith's gone to ring for the ambulance.' She squatted down on the floor, taking Shirley's head gently onto her lap. 'It's going to be all right, love,' she soothed, stroking her hair. 'We'll soon have you sorted out in the hospital.'

'Oh, Mam,' Shirley cried, looking up at her mother and trying to read her expression. Did she look as scared as Shirley felt? 'Have you seen the blood, Mam?' she gasped. 'I'm dying, aren't I? I must be! What's happening to me, Mam? *What*?'

'Shhh,' her mam said, continuing to stroke her hair. 'Hush, love. You're not dying. This is what happens when you have a baby. It's just normal. Don't you worry; it'll all be over soon, and then you'll have a bouncing baby to look after, won't you? And won't that be worth all this, eh?'

Shirley couldn't think beyond the pain and the blood on the lino, that and the exhaustion that had suddenly overtaken her. Yet she'd never felt more awake; the pain was just so bad. She tried to focus on her mam's face and draw some strength from it. It would be worth it. Of course it would. She just wanted it to be over.

Keith returned then and announced that the ambulance was on its way, but his expression at seeing the blood on the floor filled Shirley with terror all over again. She tried to wriggle herself up from the floor and sit up but felt herself being held down. 'Stay here, love,' Mary whispered into her damp hair. 'It won't be long now.' And as she did so another wave of agony gripped Shirley's body and she realised she couldn't stand if she wanted to. She heard screaming then, but wasn't even sure where it was coming from. That and the sound of sirens, getting louder and louder. Oh, just make it stop, she thought. Someone please make it stop.

The ambulance men worked like lightning getting Shirley into the back. At least, that's how it seemed – a blur of smiles and arms and blankets. But why were her mam and Keith standing there outside the ambulance looking so worried? She watched her mam pull her cardigan tightly round her middle, tucking her hands under her armpits to keep out the cold. It came to her suddenly that she'd been taken out there in the horrible pink nightie and felt a pang of embarrassment that strangers were seeing her like this. And why wasn't her mam coming? They were beginning to close the doors now. 'Mam!' she cried out as one of the men started injecting something into her arm. 'What's happening?' she asked him, panicking now. 'Why isn't my mam coming with us?'

'You'll be all right, love,' he said, smiling at her reassuringly as the engine shuddered into life. 'Your mam and your husband will be able to come later, but right now we have to get you to St Luke's, don't we?' He pointed towards her stomach. 'Get that little bugger delivered.' He then removed the needle. 'Something which will help you have a little sleep,' he explained. Shirley flinched. She hated needles, she hated blood, she hated hospitals. She felt frightened and disorientated and unable to clear her vision, and she hated losing her grip on what was happening to her most of all. *It will be worth it*, she kept telling herself as she felt herself floating. *It's all going to be worth it in the end.*

Chapter 18

When Shirley woke, the horrendous pain had gone. Disorientated and groggy now, she tried to take in her surroundings, tried to work out where she might be. There was a window directly opposite the unfamiliar bed, which she couldn't see anything out of, bar a patch of charcoal sky, and as she tried to raise herself up on the pillow to see if she could see anything more by moving, she was shocked to see a cannula taped to the back of her wrist, which was attached by a length of tubing to a drip stand by the bed.

The back of her hand stung where she'd pulled on it, and she felt achy and sore all over. And, panicking now, as the events of the morning rushed into her memory, she realised she was in a hospital bed, in some sort of side-room, all alone.

Tears began to well, even before she consciously felt tearful. 'Nurse!' she cried anxiously, feeling the panic begin to consume her. And as she gingerly lifted the crisp white sheet that covered her, she realised, with a shock, that her belly had gone down. She placed a hand over it, feeling an unfamiliar softness and fleshiness. The baby! The baby was no longer inside her. Which meant it must have been born while she slept.

She scrolled back through the scraps of things that she could remember. Of being held down by a nurse – no, it had been two nurses, hadn't it? – who were trying to quell her mounting hysteria at the intensity of the pain. And they'd spoken to her, hadn't they? Told her they were going to give her something. Something to soothe her … something to send her off to sleep. Yes, that was it – words came back to her, what the nurses had said. One nurse in particular. 'Bugger this,' she had said. Shirley recalled that exactly. 'I'm giving her another one. It's not fair she should have to go through all this.' And then nothing. They must have delivered the baby while she'd slept. She looked at the sky again. It must be evening now – perhaps later. How long *had* she slept for? It must have been hours.

She lay back again, these deductions helping her calm down a little. She'd had the baby, she'd slept and she was no longer in pain. The fear that had once again engulfed her was replaced by relief in an instant. Her baby had been born. It was *over*.

But if that were so, then where *was* her baby? She felt the fear creeping in again. Why was she lying in this bed, all alone? Was it all right? Had they taken it to an incubator or something? She tried to get out of the bed but an overwhelming nausea washed over her, and she had to lie back down for fear of being violently sick. 'Nurse!' she sobbed again, really scared again now. Where was her baby? And, for that matter, where were Keith and her mam? Why weren't they with her? Why wasn't *anyone* with her? She heard footsteps approach and pulled herself up in the bed.

A stern-looking nurse appeared in the doorway, her starched blue and white uniform instantly reassuring, despite her fixed expression; she was someone of importance, someone who could help.

'Nurse, have I had my baby?' Shirley asked hopefully, realising this was one of the nurses who'd been there, wasn't she? It was all such a blur that she couldn't quite be sure. The nurse nodded and picked up a chart from the end of the bed. 'Is it a boy or a girl? When can I see it?' Shirley asked her.

The nurse put the chart back and now she did speak. 'Look, sweetheart,' she said, and as she came closer, Shirley realised that her expression wasn't grim – it was distraught. Her mouth was set in a line not because she was being unfriendly, but because she was crying. Trying not to cry, but failing. Tears were tracking down her face. 'You had a baby boy at half past ten this morning,' she said. Then took a breath. 'But he's died, I'm afraid.' She stopped then, and came closer still, taking Shirley's hand now. 'I know it's a lot to take in, but it's a blessing in disguise, though, Shirley, *honestly* it is. The doctor'll be round … He wasn't right, my love. I'm *so* sorry. He was a thalidomide baby. Have you heard about those, Shirley? He wasn't right, and he died. But at least he's at rest now. He was never going to make it, my love. I'm so sorry, I really am.'

Shirley's head spun. What on earth was this nurse saying? What was she on about, a thalidomide baby? Heard about what? She'd heard nothing! Thalidomide was the name of the tablets she'd been taking for her morning sickness, that was all. What did they have to do with her baby?

'I want my baby,' she said again. 'His dad will be here soon, and my mam. Can you bring him to me, please?'

The nurse shook her head sadly. 'Didn't you hear me, Shirley, love?' she said gently. 'I said he *died*. There is no baby.' The tears were still plopping down, onto her cheeks, dripping off her chin, onto her uniform, and Shirley wondered distractedly if she had any babies of her own. 'But listen,' she said, 'you're a young lass, and you're healthy. There's plenty of time for more babies to come along. I'm sure it won't be long before you have another. I'll get your husband for you, shall I?' she finished. 'You'll be wanting to see him, won't you? He's here. He's still here. Only in the waiting room.' She placed the chart back on the bed end and left the room.

As she watched the nurse turn and go, Shirley started to scream. She couldn't seem to help herself. It was like she'd been taken over by something. She screamed for her baby. Why couldn't she have her baby? She'd carried him for nine months and been so careful to look after herself. What did she mean there was no baby? There had to be? She cried harder than she'd ever cried in her life, was crying so hard that when the door opened and Keith appeared, he shrank back from the noise.

And there was something else. His expression; his grey, haunted face. His eyes, which were red, and his cheeks, which were sunken, all conspired to confirm that what the nurse had said was real. That he knew exactly what had happened – was still happening now – that her baby boy, *their* baby boy, was indeed dead. That there would be no waking up from this nightmare.

'Is it true? *Is* it?' Shirley shouted at her traumatised-looking husband anyway. 'What are they on about, one of those thalidomide babies?'

Keith shrugged helplessly as he came to her and took her in his arms as best he could, taking care not to dislodge her drip. 'I only know as much as you, Shirl. They said that some women who took those sickness pills have had babies who aren't right.'

Keith tried to soothe her, but she pushed him back, angrily. 'Aren't right? What do you mean, aren't right? What was *wrong* with him?'

Keith looked wretched. Looked like he was groping for something to say. 'Shirley. It's no one's fault,' he began. 'No one's. So there's no point getting mad with me. I don't *know*. They didn't say.'

'Keith, they must have told you *something*! You don't just say a baby's not right and not say *something* about why!' Her throat was so sore and the sobs just made it hurt all the more. That was it? She was never going to see her baby, ever? Not even once? How could she let that happen? How could *Keith* let that happen? What was so wrong with the child she'd carried that they wouldn't even let her see him? 'Keith, they must have told you something!' she cried again.

Keith's expression was becoming one of mounting distress. 'Tell me,' she whispered. 'However bad it is, *tell* me!'

'Oh, *love*,' he said, 'you don't really want to know –'

'Yes, I bloody do!'

He sighed and took hold of Shirley's hand. 'They wouldn't let me see him. I did ask, but they wouldn't. Said it would be too upsetting for me …'

Shirley felt as if her heart would break into a million pieces. '*Why*? What had happened to him? What was wrong with him, Keith?'

'It was his head, they said, mostly. He had a big head,' he added quietly. 'Water on the brain. Swollen up. That's what they told me. And that –' he squeezed her free hand tightly, refusing to let her wriggle it away. 'That he didn't have proper arms or feet, Shirl. You wouldn't want to see him, that's what they said – you know, under the circumstances. Love, you wouldn't. *I* wouldn't. Like they said, I think it's for the best.'

Shirley recoiled at the image that now swam before her. She pulled her knees up and hugged them to her chest, newly anguished by the missing bulk of her distended pregnant belly – by the lack of the child she had carried inside her all these long months. But what had she given birth to? Why had it happened? What had she done to deserve such a tragedy? She rocked back and forth, crying freely, trying to pin it down to something. Was it because she'd insisted on climbing up to put those trimmings up? Her mam had told her not to, hadn't she?

Gone on and on about how she should rest? Was it the sickness? The chronic nausea that she'd never really managed to get over? How could it be the pills? They'd been all that had kept her going. How could it *possibly* be them? They were proper prescription medicine. They'd have been tested, surely? Someone would have *known* if they were dangerous. No, it couldn't have been them, could it? How could they have let something like that happen? It seemed too shocking, too unthinkable for words.

Another nurse joined them in the room then. A sister. She was carrying a kidney bowl and some paperwork and smiled sympathetically at Shirley as she placed the bowl on the locker beside the bed. It contained a square of what looked like gauze and a syringe. Were they going to put her to sleep again?

Apparently not. Not yet, at least. The nurse smiled again, if weakly. Shirley didn't smile back at her. She didn't want sympathetic smiles. She wanted her baby in her arms, whole and perfect. Not this emptiness. This horror. This inexplicable, terrible news. It was like a throbbing ache in a place she couldn't get at. 'I know you've had a shock, love,' the nurse said as she perched on the side of Shirley's bed without asking permission. 'But we need to ask something of you.' She looked down at the papers in her hand, then glanced across at Keith. 'We need your permission to let us perform a post-mortem on the baby. It's because of the thalidomide. The medicine you took for your morning sickness. There's been a few births like this up and down the country, you see, and we need to do the post-mortem to help us be sure of the cause.'

Shirley looked at Keith in shock. She knew what a post-mortem was. It meant they wanted to further mutilate her poor little boy. 'No! Keith, tell her no! They're not chopping him up as well!'

The nurse put a gentle hand on Shirley's raised knee. 'We really need to do it, love. I know it's incredibly painful for you to think about, but it's *so* important that we do it. You do see that, don't you? It's vital. It will potentially help other women in your situation,' she explained. Then she paused. 'And it might help save *their* babies.'

Shirley stared at her, even more stunned. Did the nurse think she even *cared*? Why should her precious child – her *dead* child – be chopped up? It wasn't fair! But even as her breath caught in her throat, the pain searing through her anew, she watched Keith calmly take the piece of paper and pen that were being offered to him and sign the form in his elegant handwriting. How *could* he? Frig the other mothers and frig their babies too. What about *hers*? It wasn't fair. It couldn't *be*. They might be fine, but what about her? She wanted her baby. She wanted him so badly. Wanted to take him home, to where Christmas was ready and waiting for him. To take him home and put him to bed in the crib her mam and dad had bought them. The crib with the lovely lemon blankets with a picture of a rocking horse on them. Dress him in the clothes her Granny Wiggins had already made for him. Rock him in her arms to send him to sleep. She had to have him. She didn't think she could bear to go home without him. She looked desperately towards the kidney bowl with the syringe in it. 'Oh, put me to sleep. Just put me to sleep. I don't care what you do!' She sobbed. She turned on Keith then. 'And you can bugger off as well. Go to the pub with your brothers like you usually do! Go on, get out of here and leave me alone!'

She turned her back on the pair of them as the nurse prepared her arm for the injection, and she was relieved to feel the sting of the needle piercing her skin. It would take her away, and escape was the thing she craved most now. To be taken from this hell and delivered somewhere else. To have the dreadful pictures in her head plunged into darkness. She was only vaguely aware of Keith whispering that he was leaving as she drifted off into oblivion. She didn't care.

She didn't care if she never woke up again.

Chapter 19

The Christmas of 1962 was the worst time Shirley had ever experienced in her young life. She couldn't think of a single time when she'd felt so wretched. Keith's birthday on 22 December went unmarked; it was all she could do to get out of bed and face the day. It was bad enough that her body, which was still healing after going through so much, was now so cruelly primed for feeding a newborn. She'd been given some pills to help settle her hormones, but her new curvaceous shape was almost too much to bear, so she avoided looking in mirrors. She wanted nothing more than to shrivel up and disappear. And when she did find the energy to venture out of the house, as she was constantly urged to by her mam, women with babies seemed to be everywhere, all going about their own business, proudly pushing their pink-faced sons and daughters in their lovely prams.

Mary was doing her best to console her only daughter – Shirley knew that. But in truth, because she was so grief-stricken herself, for the first couple of numb weeks she didn't really manage to help Shirley much at all, as she kept breaking down in tears herself.

Platitudes, too, came relentlessly, from every corner, so much so that they began to feel like riders on a carousel, hopping on then going round and round and round in Shirley's head: *you can try again, you're both only young, the Lord acts in mysterious ways* and, worst of all, *it was a blessing in disguise*.

A blessing in disguise? A blessing for *who* exactly? Certainly not for Shirley. And Keith wasn't much help, either. She just couldn't seem to connect with him about it at all. He just couldn't or didn't want to talk about it. It was over and done with, his weary expression seemed to say, and that was that. Whenever Shirley cried and hugged the little brown teddy bear they'd bought for the baby, Keith simply made an excuse to get out of the house. She wouldn't see him then until the early hours of the next morning, when he'd stagger back home, pissed, no use to anyone. And that was what decided it for Shirley, really. Sympathy was something she shouldn't expect, and why look for it anyway? When she got it, she didn't even know what to do with it. Nothing anyone said really spoke to her or made it better, so perhaps the best thing she could do was to simply get on with her life, and try to bury the experience somewhere in a dark recess in her mind.

It was hard to let go, though, with the fact of it ever present – and not just as a part of her physically, either. A letter came through the post on 23 December – the day after Keith's birthday had passed without comment, and two days before the day she was dreading even more. The day of their first Christmas together as a proper family. It was a letter from St Luke's Hospital, addressed to Keith, telling him he had to go back there and pay the ten pounds they owed them for 'disposing' of their first born. Shirley stared at the letter with wide, uncrying eyes. That was how bad it was; she couldn't even weep over it. Instead she reached for her purse and simply passed him the money. She knew in that moment she had lost more than her baby; she had lost a part of herself that day, too – something she knew she'd never be able to get back.

* * *

'Aren't you hungry at *all*, Shirley?' her mother asked, smiling weakly across the table at her as they sat down to their dinner on Christmas Day. They had decided on that, at least, that to stay at home would be torture. So instead they'd walked the small distance from their house to Mary and Raymond's, where they could at least sit and be tortured with company. At least, Shirley could. Was Keith suffering anything like as much as she was? She tried to force a smile on her face.

'There's just so much on my plate, Mam,' she answered. 'It's all lovely, honest. I might even save half of mine for supper.'

She turned to Keith, hoping he'd chip in and divert her mum's anxious scrutiny. 'It's lovely, isn't it?'

In answer, Keith nodded and picked up the glass of bitter Raymond had just poured from the jug. 'I tell you what, Mary, love, this is the best Christmas dinner I've ever eaten. Top notch.'

Mary's pride was visible. As was her relief. She smiled at her son-in-law. 'Aww, I'm so glad you're enjoying it, love. Our Shirley's a good cook as well, though,' she added hastily. 'I'm sure next year, when it's her turn, it'll be every bit as nice.'

Shirley tried to quash the impulse to just get up and leave them to it. It was all just so painful and it was exhausting her now. It was like having perpetual toothache.

But at least her mam had spirited away the pile of presents that had sat under the tree. She'd been so excited when Mary had shown her all the little rattles and bits and bats she'd bought earlier in the year for the baby, even if she'd scolded her at the time for going overboard and spending so much.

'Oh, don't be daft, love,' Mary had laughed, as she'd added another little something to the growing pile of Christmas gifts. 'Your dad works hard for the money, and I worked even harder to get it all off him. And what better have I to do than spend it all on my first grandchild?'

So Shirley had allowed it and indulged her mam whenever something new had appeared, understanding that, for her mam, this was a massive event as well, which would bring as much happiness to them as it would to her and Keith.

The pile was no more now, however, and the area around the tree looked horribly denuded. The brightly wrapped pile had been just a modest collection of small, adult-shaped presents: some socks and aftershave for Keith and perfume and new underwear for herself. She forced down the lump in her throat as she glanced around the table, if only to make room for a couple more mouthfuls to put her mam's mind at rest and because she knew she must make an effort not to spoil the day for everyone else. She felt it keenly, too – because they seemed to be keen to enjoy it. Could that be true? It was almost as if they'd forgotten.

When the new year blew in and Shirley could at last put Christmas to bed, she felt that sense of everyone else forgetting even more keenly. No, no one had yet said *least said soonest mended*, not that she'd heard, anyway, but she knew that was what was required of her. She was almost grateful, then, to see her GP one morning in mid-January for her check-up; at least here was somewhere she could talk about the baby she'd never seen, but who had lived and squirmed and kicked inside her, and who was still constantly at the forefront of her mind.

Shirley had been with Doctor Hardaker since she'd been a small child, and he was a bit like a favourite uncle, really. He'd had her sit for a minute while he glanced through her notes, and now he sighed as he removed his glasses and placed the file back on his big oak desk. 'Shirley, I'm so sorry about what happened, love,' he said, reaching to pat her hand almost automatically. 'The truth is that perhaps we didn't know all we should about those anti-sickness tablets, and some are saying that women shouldn't be taking them anymore.' He shifted the papers a little, and clasped his hands together on top of them. 'You know what my advice would be? Here and now? To try again, love. To have another baby, a perfect baby this time. I think the sooner you do, the sooner you'll forget all about this. Well, if not forget,' he added hastily, 'at least begin to put it all behind you. So,' he finished, 'let's have a look at you, shall we?'

Shirley stared hard at her doctor as she lay on his couch for her examination, feeling suddenly clear-sighted about it all. What was *he* sorry for? It wasn't his fault, after all. It was just one of those things, everybody had said so. Besides, Shirley thought, if she was ever to get back to any kind of normality, then she needed to put all that behind her.

Even so, she hadn't even thought about trying again just yet. In fact, the opposite was true. She was still grieving for the baby she'd carried but never held, not thinking about making a replacement. Wasn't it much, much too soon?

Not that any of that sexy stuff held any interest for her right now, anyway – it was the very last thing on her mind. She'd had lots of stitches from where the forceps had torn her, and her body was still healing – just thinking about them still made her wince. The more she thought about it now, though, the more it suddenly made sense to try again. Perhaps another baby would help fill the hole in her heart. Perhaps another baby would make everything better, and mean that people wouldn't have to tip-toe around her any more. It might mean she could get back to normal and feel whole again.

'Thank you, doctor,' she said when he'd finished feeling her tummy, 'I think that's exactly what I'll do.'

'Good lass,' the doctor said, smiling. 'Let's get a smile back on that pretty face.'

Keith was both surprised and very grateful. Not least because he was suddenly back to being flavour of the month *and* there was no need to make a dent in their precious finances or borrow money off Granny Wiggins for contraceptives. Granny Wiggins had been firm on that point. She'd even taken Shirley aside to discuss 'women's issues' with her, getting her to promise she'd not even think of trying for another child until she was completely fit and well again – both in her body and in her mind. 'And don't you worry about paying for the contraceptive pill,' she'd told Shirley. 'I'll see to all that for you.'

Shirley had been grateful, even if she hadn't planned on taking her granny up on it, but now the visit to the doctor's had changed everything. The answer to her pain was clearly to try as soon as possible. So, buoyed by his blessing, she went straight home to Keith and announced they'd start trying right away.

It didn't take long for her to fall pregnant. Within three weeks, prompted by a familiar nausea, she went back to the doctor's to have a blood test, and it confirmed it – there was indeed a second baby on the way.

Shirley didn't allow herself to be consumed by this pregnancy, however. She didn't dare. She'd entered a new world now, a world in which bad things could happen, and she didn't want to tempt fate by letting her mind wander – if she did, she'd find herself thinking 'when' rather than 'if', when there was a very big 'if' river to cross. Though she didn't go back to work – if she was going to be sick all the time, it wouldn't be possible anyway, and again, supported by her mam, she remained at home. And as she hadn't been back to work yet, she decided that it was safer to stay as she was. It meant that Keith had to work extra hard and take up a few decorating jobs at weekends, but she figured it would be worth it and she didn't want to take any chances. Fate was now her enemy, and she was determined to head it off. She asked her mam to promise that she wouldn't start going out and buying things, and to store everything she already had down at her house.

'Shirley, it's your second chance,' Mary told her, 'and you need to stop worrying about it. Lightning doesn't strike twice, and you need to stop worrying. I'll keep all the things if you want me to, course I will, love. But everything will be fine this time. You'll see.'

'Yes, Mam, I *do*,' Shirley said, resolute that she must do nothing to jinx this pregnancy. 'Annie told me we should never have bought the pram in the first place. She said it's bad luck to bring a pram home before the baby, so I want to do it right this time.'

'That Annie's too superstitious for her own good,' Mary had huffed. But it made no difference to Shirley. Everything she could do, she would do. That was the only way to quash the nagging sense that refused to leave her, that it might have been something she'd done or not done that had made her baby son die as soon as he'd been born.

Shirley didn't know what to do about Keith, though. She'd thought he'd be excited about the new baby she was expecting, but it seemed as if the opposite was true. And it hurt her. Didn't he care? He didn't act like he did. In fact, he seemed to want to go out more than ever. Heading off to the pub with either his brothers or his friends, and, when he was home, refusing to even acknowledge Shirley was pregnant. Did he wish she wasn't? Was that it? It certainly seemed so.

'You can't let him get away with it,' Mary warned Shirley one morning, after Keith had been out yet again with his brothers. And while he was at home sleeping off yet another hangover (when he was supposed to be at work), she'd gone down to her mam's for some company. 'You need to put your foot down, love. Before it's too late.'

'I can't, Mam,' Shirley said. 'He just doesn't listen. It's okay if I never mention being pregnant, but the minute I say anything about it, that's it – he's off down to the bookies or up to the pub. I'm getting sick of it, I really am.'

'You listen to me, Shirley,' Mary said. 'All men are the same. If you let them get away with murder, then they will. It's up to us women to change things. Always was. Why should the men do what they like? It's all wrong. No, I'm telling you, Shirley, the next time he gets ready for the pub, you get yourself dolled up and you bloody well go with him. Oh, they don't mind putting you in the club, but trust me, love – when they've given you a belly full of arms and legs, they'd sooner be eyeing up some slim slut down the pub and leave you tied to the kitchen sink. Don't fall for it, I'm telling you.'

Shirley flinched to hear her mam talking like that. She really didn't think her Keith was that sort of man, but what if her mam was right? What if he was looking around? Maybe she had been letting herself go a bit lately – she'd had so much else on her mind, after all. Was that why he always wanted to be out of the house?

Perhaps she needed to do what her mam suggested.

'Run me a bath, love, while you're in there,' she shouted into the tiny bathroom where Keith was shaving at the sink, the following Friday evening. 'I'm going to get myself ready and come with you for a change. It's ages since I've been out for a drink. Or seen any of our friends, for that matter. And I'm sick of staring at these four walls while you go out gallivanting,' she finished

Keith stepped out onto the landing and stared at her, the bottom half of his face covered in soap. 'What are you frigging on about?' he asked.

'I'm coming with you,' she said. 'You're out all the time, Keith, and if I want to go out as well then I bloody will!'

His expression was so shocked by this that it only served to fuel her anger. 'Have you got someone else on the go already, is that it? You have, haven't you? That's what it is, isn't it? It's because I'm getting fat again, isn't it?' She couldn't stop herself then – she started pummelling at him, raining blows against his chest.

Keith grabbed a towel and tried to wipe it across his chin while defending himself from her blows at the same time. He then grabbed her arms and pulled her firmly towards his chest. 'Don't be stupid, you daft mare. You sound just like your frigging mother! What on earth put an idea like that in your head?'

Shirley only sobbed harder. It was almost as if her mam was there with her. 'You're never in the house, Keith! And you won't ever talk about the baby with me – *ever*! And you've stopped taking me out. What am I *supposed* to think?'

Keith dropped his arms, his expression shocked. And it made her stop hitting him. It was as if one of her physical blows had connected, even though it hadn't. 'Don't say that, Shirley,' he said quietly. 'Please don't say that. You have no idea, do you?'

Shirley caught her breath then, suddenly afraid of what she might hear. What was he talking about? 'Come on then,' she said, gathering herself. 'Enlighten me then, Keith. You might as well tell me now and get it over with.'

Keith's head snapped up, his eyes boring into her face. But it was several seconds before he spoke. 'You think it's been easy for me, all this, do you?' he said finally, still holding her. 'Well, it hasn't. You think I don't care that my son was born dead and buried within 12 hours? A son I wasn't even allowed to see? My son – a kid I watched you carry for me for nine months, and then ... nothing. And then seeing you there, not knowing – knowing I'd have to try and explain to you. Tell you things I didn't want to know and didn't want to tell you.' He took a breath and wiped the towel over his face again before continuing. 'Now, I'm not saying it isn't right, Shirley, because it is. Of course it is. But let's be honest, it's been hard for me as well. And I don't have a mam to run to, do I? My job's to shut up and get on with it – that's what everyone's been saying, Shirley. Be strong. Get her to buck up – act like it's all going to be okay this time. Course they do! I'm a man, after all, aren't I? Well you know what?' he said. 'Never again. That's what I've been thinking, if I'm honest. I can't cope with it. I'm not sure I can go through it again, Shirley. Seeing what it's put you through. I just can't. It's tearing me up inside. And I'm sorry if that makes me a prat. It's just the way it is.'

Shirley stared at her husband, stunned, not knowing what to think, much less what to say. She sat down on the top step of the stairwell and dropped her head into her hands. Her mam had been wrong. So wrong. Why hadn't she *seen* that? All men were *not* the same. How had she been blind to that, too? How had she not given Keith a second thought during her tragedy – *their* tragedy? She felt terrible even thinking it. How had she not given a thought to how awful it must have been for him as well? Worse, in some ways – because she'd slept through it, drugged up, oblivious. While poor Keith, who, as well as worrying about the baby, must have been terrified about what might happen to *her*, as well. Who'd had to live through it, hear the news, know he had to face her when she woke, knowing that her heart would be broken.

He was right. It had all been about her, all the time. And there'd been no one for him, *no one*. He'd just had to put on a brave face. When, in fact, he wasn't feeling brave at all.

'I'm sorry, Keith,' she whispered as he came and sat down beside her. 'I … I just … well, I just thought you didn't really *care*.'

Keith put his arm around her. 'It's all right, love. I know it was worse for you. I just didn't know how to deal with it – I still don't. I really don't. I'm not good with letting it all out, Shirl – you know that. I never have been. But that doesn't mean I don't feel it. Because I do.'

Shirley hugged him tight. She no longer cared about going tit for tat with this man. Her mam was wrong.

'Go on, Keith,' she sniffed. 'Go get ready and go for a few pints. You need them. I'm fine. I think I'll get an early night instead.'

Keith kissed the top of her head. 'You know what?' he said. 'I'm not really in the mood now. How about we have a night in, just the two of us?' He laughed softly. 'No, sorry – just the *three* of us,' he corrected. 'Fish and chips. Feet up. Watch the telly. How about doing that instead?'

Shirley nodded. That would do her fine. Well, she thought, feeling the 'morning' sickness making its presence felt yet again, apart from the fish.

But their good fortune wasn't to last. One week after their first wedding anniversary, on 17 March, Shirley woke up from a nap feeling something horribly familiar clenching in her stomach and a warm stickiness that took her straight back to the events of the previous December. By the end of the night, while Keith sat in the pub with his brother, oblivious, she'd clutched her tummy and said goodbye to her second baby, wondering as she wept what she or Keith could have possibly done to deserve such wretchedness.

Chapter 20

20 April 1964

Monday's child is fair of face,
Tuesday's child is full of grace,
Wednesday's child is full of woe,
Thursday's child has far to go,
Friday's child is loving and giving,
Saturday's child must work for a living,
But the child that's born on the Sabbath day,
Is fair and wise and good and gay.

Just over a month after her and Keith's second wedding anniversary, Shirley was being carted off to the labour ward at St Luke's Hospital. Doctor Hardaker had insisted that this time there would be no mistakes. 'The minute you feel that first pain, Shirley,' he told her at her last appointment, 'you send someone to ring for an ambulance as quick as you can.' He'd taken her hand to reassure her then. 'I promise, love,' he said, 'it's going to be third time lucky, you wait and see.'

Shirley hadn't been convinced she'd be lucky ever again. Yes, she'd been lucky in love, but was she ever going to become a mother? She really didn't dare hope. All those months carrying another infant had brought back such painful memories; it had almost felt like she had held her breath for the entire pregnancy. It was so hard to shoo away the images lodged in her brain – of all the blood, the terrible pain, the being put to sleep and waking up to find her longed-for child wasn't with her, of the nurse coming in and telling her things she couldn't bear to hear, of being told her tiny baby had been 'disposed of'.

'Are you *sure* there's no chance of them tablets still being in my system this time?' She'd asked Dr Hardaker that, again and again. There'd been so much talk about the sickness tablets since she'd lost her son, and it was talk she found difficult to listen to. But that hadn't stopped her taking it in. Ever since her miscarriage the previous year she had been convinced that the same tablets that had meant her first baby had been born deformed had also been responsible for her losing her second. Who knew what they'd done to her? Who knew what they'd damaged? And though no one had ever admitted it in public, Dr Hardaker had even hinted at it himself. 'Yes,' he'd admitted, after she'd had her miscarriage, 'until we know all the facts about thalidomide I can't rule out that they might have played a part in what happened.'

And it was too late for her in any case, so she could only try to look forward. She had suffered her morning sickness with stoicism. And today, with only the last hurdle to jump, remembering his confidence was reassuring. 'There's *nothing* in your system, Shirley, I promise,' he'd said, in answer to her question, every time. 'You've nothing to be afraid of. And you've been fit and healthy throughout this pregnancy, so *please* don't worry yourself.'

But how could she not worry? It wasn't just her, either. Keith had too – he'd been getting more and more distant again. The rounder she had become, the more he'd withdrawn from her – and even her mam was like a nervous wreck.

All the things that had been bought for the much longed-for first baby had now been given away. Shirley had been adamant that they didn't go to family, either, for fear that they might bring bad luck. And she'd stuck to it, only being persuaded to change her mind when Keith's Malcolm and his wife Valerie had had their baby Steven. 'Go on, Shirl,' Annie had said to her, 'let them have them if you're getting rid of them. You know how strapped for cash they are – they'd be so grateful for a cot and pram.'

And they had been, and though Valerie clearly had some reservations, they weren't about superstition – they were about how Shirley might feel about it when she was still without a baby of her own.

'You *sure* about this, love?' Valerie had asked when Keith and Raymond had carried them from the car as they dropped them off for her.

'Course I am,' Shirley had told her. 'It's good to keep them in the family.' But it didn't stop her worrying that she might have jinxed them in some way. How could she not feel like that, given what had happened to her?

But then she'd fallen pregnant for a third time and it was as if everyone around her breathed a sigh of relief. And then, almost as soon as they'd done that, they all started holding their breath all over again. And however much everyone told her it would be all right this time, she knew that privately everyone was as terrified as she and Keith were – not daring to count any chickens until they'd well and truly hatched.

All bar Keith's Margaret, who proved the best tonic imaginable. As Shirley's date drew near, she and Bob even came across from Preston, and, in honour of their visit, despite Shirley being so heavily pregnant, she was adamant that there was no question of them sleeping downstairs. They'd have the double bed upstairs, Shirley insisted, while she and Keith made the best of it down in the living room, because, in truth, she told Margaret, she could no longer get comfortable in bed anyway. She was just so grateful for Margaret's calm, reassuring presence. Of all the loved ones around her, she knew Margaret understood how she felt.

Margaret's refusal to fuss was like a breath of fresh air. 'She's bleeding pregnant – not an invalid!' she would point out to anyone who dared to try step in and tell Shirley she shouldn't be doing this or that, or – the thing she hated most – treated her like a porcelain doll. She even managed to shut up Shirley's mam – the worst culprit – something Shirley had barely ever seen anyone do before, which only served to raise Margaret further in her eyes.

Her mam had called round to see if they needed anything from the shop, and when she saw Shirley wringing out Keith's shirt in the sink, she went mad.

'Bloody leave that for him to do when he gets home!' she had snapped. 'Who's he think he is, having you sort his dirty laundry, you in your state!' She then tried to get between Shirley and the sink, and bustle her across the room to sit down.

Margaret, who'd been sitting on the couch sewing a hem, stood straight up.

'Mary, love,' she said mildly, 'I know you're Shirley's mother, but you're really not doing her any favours keeping her from her jobs. Our Keith's at work all day, and he's not going to want to come home to a sinkful, is he? Honestly, Mary, just think – they have it easy these days, don't they? Remember when we had kids? None of them pain-killing injections and stuff back then, was there? None of all that "sit down and rest" malarkey, was there? And them poor bloody Indian women just squat down in the woods, don't they? Have their babies then get straight on with their work. No, love,' she said, while Shirley stood there, open-mouthed, 'leave her be. She needs to get *used* to being busy now, being run off her feet.' She grinned at Shirley. 'Now she's going to be a mum, like you and me.'

Mary had gaped at Margaret, and Shirley could see the point had been made. It also confirmed her instinct that it was Margaret she needed at her side when the day came.

So when the pains started rippling through her at half past six that morning, she left Keith snoring on the carpet and crept upstairs.

'Margaret,' she whispered urgently as she shook her sister-in-law awake. 'I think the baby's on its way.'

Margaret sat up immediately, as if she'd only been in the lightest of sleeps. 'Are you sure, love?' she said. 'Are you having labour pains?'

Shirley had never seen Margaret looking anything less than perfect, and looking at her now – devoid of make-up and her hair looking like a scarecrow's – brought a smile to her face, despite the pain. '*Yes*,' she confirmed, 'I've been having them for a couple of hours now – least, I think so – but I'm scared, Margaret. I don't know if I dare go to the hospital. Not after last time. I think I'd rather have it here.'

Margaret tutted as she threw the covers back and swung her legs out of the bed. 'Don't be silly, love,' she whispered briskly. 'You go back downstairs while I get dressed. Is our Keith awake?'

Shirley shook her head. 'No,' she said, 'not yet.'

'Well, it's time he was then,' Margaret said, 'so get yourself back downstairs and have him get the kettle on while I get dressed, so we can have a cup of tea at least before we call the ambulance.'

Shirley did as she was told, wincing as another contraction gripped her in the kitchen, wondering whether she should send for her mam. She decided not to; not yet, at any rate – she didn't want her mam's usual fuss and flap today. She just wanted to stay calm.

Keith, on the other hand, didn't have a calm bone in his body. In fact, Margaret had to threaten to slap him if he didn't sit still and shut up.

'But we need to call the ambulance!' he kept insisting. 'I need to go and call for it!'

'No, you *don't*,' Margaret kept answering. 'It's too soon. You call it now and all poor Shirl will end up doing is hanging around the bleeding hospital for hours on end.'

'So I'll go and call the ambulance and tell them to leave it for half an hour, then!'

'Keith!' Margaret snapped. 'It's a bleeding ambulance! Not a taxi cab. You phone them and they come. There and then. Soon as possible. You don't bleeding *book* them in advance!' She trained steely eyes on his. 'Now, if you can't do anything *helpful*, then go for a pissing walk or something, will you?'

With the pains worsening with every cycle, Shirley wished Keith *would* get the frigging ambulance, not least because the offer of a nice cup of tea didn't even seem to include her. 'Trust me, Shirley,' Margaret said, 'you can't have *anything* to eat or drink yet. Just in case they have to knock you out or something.'

'What, *anything*?' Shirley squawked. 'Not even a drink of water?'

Margaret shook her head. 'Sorry, love. Not even water. My Bob's mate's an ambulance man, so I know that for a fact.'

There was nothing for it, then, but to pace, gripping various pieces of furniture as and when required, all the while groaning in agony and waiting until Keith and her guests had all finished their morning cuppa. By now, Bob had joined them downstairs, as well, and, almost as if in solidarity, he was stumbling about like she was: since they'd last visited, his eyesight had progressively worsened, and now he couldn't see very well at all.

Not that Margaret was prepared to give him any quarter. 'Jesus Christ, Keith!' she said, watching her husband stumbling around, trying to find a seat, 'Have you *seen* these two? Now I know what they mean when they say it's like the blind leading the blind!'

She then burst out into great peals of laughter. And Shirley smiled, despite the pain. She was definitely the right person to have around.

But now she was at the hospital, the pains coming thick and fast, the fear of what was to come eclipsed everything. She'd gone on her own – the ambulance men insisting that there wasn't room for anyone else – and now that she was being transferred to the delivery suite, she didn't think she'd ever felt so alone. Not even her mam – who all of a sudden she wanted more than anything – would be allowed in to help and hold her hand.

And worse than anything was that Sister Harris, the midwife, kept shouting at her. Yes, she added 'love' on the end of each utterance, but if she thought that made it better she was wrong. 'Push, love! You have to push, love! You can do much better than that, love!' But she couldn't. She was pushing so hard that her eyes were almost popping out.

'I can't,' Shirley wept. 'I just can't do it anymore.'

Considering what she'd already gone through with her two previous pregnancies, nothing had prepared Shirley for this kind of trauma. This relentless pain, this endless shouting, this refusal by anyone to accept that she *just couldn't do it anymore!* She'd been in full-blown labour for five and a half hours now, and she was too knackered to carry on. Why couldn't they just let her sleep for a while? Build her strength up? Have another try tomorrow? The midwife, when she suggested this, burst out laughing, as did her junior. Which at least made them seem a bit more human.

'Oh, love,' she said, 'I know you're tired, sweetheart, and I know what you've already been through, but I'm afraid that there's no going back now – no way of stopping things. Much as I'd love to put my feet up and have a cuppa and a currant bun back in the office, this baby's coming whether we like it or not.'

Shirley was getting nausous now with the amount of gas and air she'd been using, and she was beginning to feel as though she was out of her own body and watching some other poor exhausted woman trying to push her baby out. 'I can't do it!' she screamed with the next powerful contraction. 'You have to help me.'

Sister Harris looked at Shirley's chart and then took her temperature. 'I won't be a second, Shirley, love, I'm going to speak to the doctor.'

As soon as she left, Shirley was gripped by a feeling of pure terror. What was happening now? What did Sister Harris know that she didn't? Was she going to come back with a syringe and put her to sleep again? Was she going to wake up in another living hell?

It seemed not. Though the doctor now at her beside looked concerned, he had no needle – just an air of brisk efficiency.

'Don't worry, Mrs Hudson,' he told her in his deep, no-nonsense voice, 'it just seems that the baby is ready to say hello, and we need to give you a bit of a hand.'

He then turned the midwife who had been stroking Shirley's hand. 'Forceps,' he told her. 'Please prepare the stirrups.'

To Shirley's horror, her legs were suddenly dragged even further apart and placed in loops of canvas slung from straps either side of the bed. Stirrups was right, she thought, trying to still her racing heartbeat, though still finding space in her head to feel eternally grateful that husbands weren't allowed in the delivery room. But the moment was fleeting; it was only seconds before the pain between her legs became so intense and unbearable that she thought she was going to pass out.

But just as her head started spinning into space, she heard the unmistakable sound of a baby's cry. The midwife checked her watch and then stroked the damp wisps of hair from Shirley's face. 'It's a baby girl, Shirley. A flipping big one, an' all!'

The pain disappeared as if spirited away on horseback. Gone, all of it. *Gone*. It felt like the biggest miracle imaginable. 'Is she all right? Is she okay?' she asked. 'What day is it?'

Sister Harris beamed at her. She really wasn't so bad, after all. 'Why, it's her birthday, of course,' she told her. 'And it's a Monday, love, remember? And, let me see, Monday's child is fair of face, isn't she? And, oh, she really *is*. And she has ten little fingers and ten little toes – I counted. So don't you worry. She is absolutely *fine*.'

As Margaret, Keith and Mary later crowded around the little white-blanketed bundle that Shirley was cradling, she could hardly believe anyone on earth could be as happy as she was at that moment. Just looking at her husband gazing so tenderly at the daughter they'd created was, without a doubt, the best feeling in the world. 'I thought of a name, love,' she told him. 'As long as that's all right with you. Is it?'

Margaret laughed. 'Shirley, love,' she said, before he'd even opened his mouth, 'you should have seen his face when he phoned and they told him you'd had her. He was like a bleeding dog with two tails. I don't think he'll give two hoots *what* you want to call her.'

'She's so beautiful, love,' Mary whispered as she gazed at her first grandchild. 'I had a look at all them other new babies on my way in, and they looked all wrinkly and screwed up. Our little girl here is by *far* the prettiest.'

'Oh, Mam, honestly!' Shirley said, realising she had a lifetime of this ahead and not minding at all. 'Will you give up? *All* babies are beautiful.'

Keith shook his head. 'Your mam's right. Not as beautiful as this one is, Shirl,' he said. 'As she would be,' he added proudly. 'She's a Hudson. Anyway, you were saying. What *did* you want to call her, love?'

My mam got her way, of course. They named me Julie.

Epilogue

Shirley and Keith went on to have two more children after me – Glenn in 1965 and Paula in 1967. After that Shirley decided to get sterilised as, despite her childhood desire to have 'lots and lots' of children, they thought that three were probably enough.

In 1968 they re-married. The way of the Hudsons had always been to send their kids to Catholic school, and as Shirley didn't want to disrespect their tradition, she and Keith got wed again, this time in the local Catholic church, so that their own three Hudson children could attend St Anthony's RC School in Clayton.

During the 1970s, the family moved back to Canterbury estate for a while, as Keith was determined that his kids learn to look after themselves, believing that village life produced children that didn't know nearly enough about *real* life. He taught all three of them to box at an early age, just as his dad had with him, and if any of them ever got bullied – boy or girl – either he or Shirley would drag them out to the street and insist they fight their corner, win or lose.

Keith's mam, Annie, never settled in a home of her own again, preferring to move around members of her huge extended family, and making her presence felt right to the last. In late August 1980 she was staying with her sister Mary's daughter, Gloria, and, true to form, getting impatient waiting for the local club to open so she could go and get a drink.

Gloria, busy styling her hair for her, as she often did, was trying hard to talk her into waiting for an extra hour and going down with her and her husband.

'If you just hang on till seven o'clock, Auntie Annie,' she said, 'then me and Wilf will walk you.'

'I'm not a bleeding invalid, Glo!' Annie had snapped. 'And you know as well as I do that the club opens at *six*. Now just hurry up with my bleeding hair and don't leave a bald spot showing like you did last night!'

At a quarter past six, Annie, by now 76, ordered a whisky at the bar of the New Roadside Club in Low Moor. She took her usual seat, a sip of her drink and then died at the table.

In 1985, Shirley's mam, Mary Read, also died. Aged only 66, she had been suffering from dementia for the last two years of her life when she finally died in hospital of a brain aneurysm. That was in June. In October of the same year, Raymond joined his beloved wife. He was also 66 and died of lung cancer. Shirley was distraught at losing both parents so quickly and had a terrible time coming to terms with it.

Keith and Shirley – my lovely mum and dad – are now in their seventies, and still as much in love as they ever were. It's been many years now, but on 14 December every year they remember their lost baby boy, and wonder. Despite trying, they have been unable to find out where he was buried, and, at the time of writing, no one has taken responsibility for his death.

Acknowledgements

I would like to thank my agent Andrew Lownie for this wonderful opportunity to tell my stories, and the team at HarperCollins for putting their trust in me every step of the way. I also want to thank the wonderful Lynne Barrett-Lee for helping me turn my dream into reality. Without her help, these stories would still be in the box in my garage, gathering dust.

I would like to dedicate these books first and foremost to my parents Keith and Shirley Hudson. They made me who I am today, and have loved and supported me all my life. And to my gorgeous husband Ben, who has had to endure me practically ignoring him for two years while I worked on my writing, and who learned how to cook, clean and work the washing machine while I was in my 'zone'. I also need to mention my brother Glenn and sister Paula, who have giggled along with me as I decided what material to use and what most definitely needed to stay buried, and my cousin Susan Taylor (our Nipper), who has been on hand whenever I needed her for historical accuracy or juicy snippets. All of my family deserve a mention, but they are legion and mentioning them all would fill a book. They know how much I love them.

Finally, I also dedicate all these words to my favourite ever cousin, Willie Jagger. Rest in peace, Willie. You know how much you're loved and no doubt you'll be laughing your arse off up there at the thought of me being an author. Every time I see our Pauline it makes me so happy because she reminds me of everything you were.